D1563532

# I AM _____:

## The Untold Story of Success

KLYN ELSBURY

*Edited by*

RIC GROEBER

*With Special Foreword from*
LARRY LINNE,
former NFL wide receiver, author,
CEO, and entrepreneur

"*A bird sitting on a*
*branch is never afraid*
*of it breaking, because her trust isn't*
*in the branch, but her own wings.*"

- unknown

# Dedication

With love, I dedicate this book to all of the influencers in the world: past, present, and future. May you trust your own wings and soar to new places.

# A special dedication

To my editor, Ric Groeber, for the tireless devotion to this mission.

To all of the influencers featured, for the open and honest inquiry into the depths of their souls.

To my mother and father, Ann and Burdette Elsbury, for giving me a loving home and a supportive environment.

And to the love of my life, who reminds me every day that life isn't always about how many breaths we take, but about living for the moments that take our breath away.

# Contents

# *Foreword by*
# LARRY LINNE
By former NFL wide receiver, author,
and CEO of InCite Performance Group

A troubled child is keeping you up at night.

Your job is frustrating and your clients are being unreasonable.

Your boss is threatening you and now you're worried you may not be employed in the near future.

Your spouse tells you they are leaving you.

You are exhausted from the complexity of life, and don't know if things will ever change.

This list goes on...


Isn't it amazing how life can throw so many things at us? Sometimes those things seem insurmountable. If we are fortunate, they eventually pass or become diluted issues in our life, and we are ok again. But then, just as we begin to move on, another thing comes upon us to bring us down again.

You might think to yourself, "Why does everyone else seem so together... so in charge of their life... so in control?" How are they getting the good luck and the good breaks?

My experience tells me that they are not so lucky. Most people have adversity in their lives, for the majority of their lives. Unfortunately, many people succumb to their adversities which cause them to stop progressing and stop reaching for exciting and high level dreams. Their challenges cause them to quit... to give up... to accept lesser outcomes, or even give up completely.

When Klyn Elsbury first called me and asked if she could interview me, I didn't know why. She quickly described her intentions of "interviewing successful business people and athletes to find out what made each person so successful". Of course I was flattered and immediately let my ego think of all the big things I could brag about. I was a highly accomplished professional athlete, successful CEO, award winning author, and have made a very good income. On top of that, I have an amazing marriage and have raised beautiful kids.

But, my mind quickly shot to the problems I have experienced in my life as well, including the difficulties I've had with my kids, marriage, work, and all the times I have failed. Why was I worthy? So many others have much greater stories. My mind became very scattered as I spoke with her. As we continued to converse, I started to realize that success is very difficult to define. It means something different to every person. I finally came to my own conclusion that success is our ability to avoid and overcome adversity.

It's not about a certain dollar amount, specific award or prize, or a cool job title. Success is doing what most aren't willing to do. It is to overcome adversity and move on to the next challenge. The ladder of success is a constant challenge of taking on each oncoming hurdle and punching it in the mouth. As terrible as this may sound, it has rewards and satisfaction that is much greater than dropping back into the lower steps of the ladder and accepting defeat. When people give in to difficulty and challenge, they drop into a pool of depression and dissatisfaction in life.

These realizations were reinforced to me as I continued to collaborate with Klyn. She took on the certainty of the end of her life and emerged as a dominant victor. She has incredible stories of overcoming both the pain and sicknesses she was battling, along with the overwhelming financial cost of her illness.

As I spoke with Klyn, I went online to learn a bit more about her and what she has gone through. She was a fitness trainer? What? How could this be? She had been on multiple national media interviews! What? How did a "sick girl" who was in the hospital more than anyone I have ever known become so healthy, famous, and successful?

Everything came into perspective as I continued to hear her story and hear about how she has never accepted failure, or let it be the end of her story. She never let "No" stop her from anything that mattered, or in her potential to meet her goals.

I granted her the interview. I told her reasons why I was successful as an athlete, business executive, father, husband, and a few other things. The strategies, beliefs, discipline, and passion that allowed me to be so lucky to have a few things to brag about flowed off my tongue.

Klyn was so genuinely interested and excited about every item I shared. She told me how so many people she had interviewed said very similar, or even the exact same things I had shared. She was finding some magic keys to why some people are successful and why others may not have such good luck. She asked great questions and extracted things that I was proud to share.

The entire time we spoke, I couldn't get out of my mind what an incredible young woman she was. I felt like a high school basketball player being interviewed by Michael Jordan! Klyn had accomplished things nobody else had ever done. Nobody! And the challenges she faced were things people said were impossible! The NFL is difficult to reach, but not impossible. Great wealth is only accomplished by a few, but it is also not impossible. Titles, victories, and all the things you will read in this book are things that can be achieved. None of them should ever be considered impossible.

Klyn herself is perhaps the greatest story of this book because she accomplished the impossible... twice. My bet is that she will accomplish more impossible things in her life because she fears nothing and is always learning. She changed the rules for battling Cystic Fibrosis. She beat insurance companies and big pharma. She looks at life as a gift and lives it fuller than anyone I had ever seen. Klyn is learning everything she can from others so she can find her next success. She is bold and willing to call and interview successful people so she can continue her quest for success, and to share her strategy with the world.

Reading about ex NFL athletes and successful business executives certainly will give insights to what it takes to be great. Obtaining the view from Klyn Elsbury is a priceless strategy for reaching your highest potential.

Read this book and redefine who you are and who you will be. "I Am ___: The Untold Story of Success".

# A Letter

*To the Present and Future Entrepreneurs,*
*Athletes, and Achievers of Our World,*

The following story was all started by one disease, the genetic killer, Cystic Fibrosis. It's partially my battle between loving to laugh and my fear of the coughing fit that ensues when I do. It's my battle in searching for moments that take my breath away, while my lungs struggle to fill with air.

It's a long story and at times, not a pretty one. It's raw. It's emotional. In order to tell it, I had to put myself in my parent's heads to imagine what it must be like to sit down and plan my funeral while they are bedside watching a machine breathe for me.

In my darkest days, I packed my suitcase for the emergency room full of clothes, nail polish, makeup, a homemade blanket from high school, and books. When I didn't have friends visiting, I had mentors coaching me, although they never knew it. Whenever a doctor told me that I lost a large portion of my lung function due to infection, I turned to my books where coaches like Darren Hardy, Napoleon Hill, Rick Pitino, Larry Winget, Malcolm Gladwell, Robert Kiyosaki and Sharon Lechter all kept me company. I felt that for me to leave any impact on this world, especially if statistically I only had a few years left, I needed to condition myself to think like they thought.

After years of this conditioning, I noticed common threads throughout the mindsets of today's household names. I began to see how entrepreneurs, athletes, and high achievers view the world around them, and that was how I started viewing my life in the hospital. Those "vacations at Club Med" became a spiritual awakening for me. I had two weeks of uninterrupted meditation time every two months. I packed my suitcase with countless books and highlighters and became a student and their secret groupie.

I have such a love for entrepreneurs and athletes and how they play life's game. The way achievers view the world, the process and habits they form to pursue what they want, and the "why" behind their ambition even when things aren't going so smoothly. I love their constant paradigm shifts, their unpredictability, and the endless sports analogies relating to business (that embarrassingly, I had to go home and Google). I know out of their darkest days, came the brightest sunrises. I firmly believe that when they lose everything (and a surprisingly high number have), they will win it all back.

Then came my opportunity. In the summer of 2015 I authored a blog that went viral. The success of this blog ultimately took me on a journey that included appearances on several national news reports and winning a battle against insurance companies for the entire state of California. This led to fan mail... fan mail from parents who now truly believe they can see their kids graduate high school...fan mail from teenage girls who believe they now will live long enough to meet prince charming and get married...fan mail from parents who know their child now has the possibility to outlive them. All of my wishes came true because of the philosophy and mindset I learned along the way.

When I was first approached about writing a book, I was encouraged to create a memoir on dying with a terminal illness. However, my life is far from over and "terminal" does not describe my mindset. Cystic Fibrosis will not kill me in a year. I'm no longer actively planning out the last few years of my life. I have not updated my will. We all pass, but it's just not my time. What the world needs is not a gut-wrenching story about negative aspects of living in a hospital for months out of the year. What the world needs is a better place to wake up every morning. As Senator Brian Nieves said, "This is a story that needs to be told", but instead of it being about me...it's about the way we all win the game.

Much love from your biggest fan,
Klyn Elsbury

Chapter 1

# The Power of Failure

One night back in the summer of 2015 I was wrapped in a blanket, lying on top of an RV off of a scenic overlook in Utah staring up at a sky full of endless, scintillating stars. The air was cool and crisp, delightfully tickling my lungs as they adjusted to the altitude. A handsome man with a beautiful soul was holding my hand and pointing out Venus to the south. Together, we were dreaming about the future. Something that until recently, I had all but given up on.

A few years earlier I had dropped out of college because I was being hospitalized several times a year, and I believed I would never live long enough to pay off my student loan debt. After my stint at college, I moved to Florida, and then to California for a career in biotech/pharmaceutical recruiting so I could be closer to the companies that were developing the very drugs that would keep me alive. Working in that industry gave me hope. When I started getting hospitalized every four months, I made the choice to leave my corporate career and preserve my lung function via exercise, diet, and adherence to prescriptions that managed the symptoms. I tried to get accepted for every clinical trial for Orkambi, before it was even called Orkambi, but time and time again I was denied because my lung function was too unstable.

He squeezed my hand excitedly, "did you see that?" referring to a shooting star that emblazoned an almost pitch black night. My heart skipped a beat. I shut my eyes and made a wish that someday soon, I would be on this drug. I opened my eyes and saw him smiling back at me. For the first time in a long time, I believed I would have a future again.

About a month ago, when Orkambi was first approved, I was the first person in clinic. However, the doctors couldn't write a prescription because I needed to go on IV antibiotics first. My lung function was around 50%. This was my third round of IVs this year alone. Meanwhile, one of my girlfriends locally who got approved for the drug posted on Facebook that for the first time in years, she woke up without coughing. I can't imagine a morning where an alarm clock wakes me up instead of a violent core-shaking, gut busting cough.

"Wow!" We both said in unison at yet, another shooting star. Who is lucky enough to see two of them in one-night sky just moments apart? Surely this means there are good things to come. Waking up without a cough became my second wish.

A week before taking off on this road trip, I finished my final round of IV treatment. As soon as it was complete, I went to my clinic for an evaluation. After three weeks of intense IV's, my blood tests revealed my kidneys and liver were strong enough to start Orkambi. I just had to fill out two simple forms, and then they would fax it in for me. Simple.

The first fax was never received. I called the clinic. They sent it again. This back and forth continued seven times. Finally, my form went through. I had my initial phone call with Orkambi's maker, Vertex, somewhere between the drive from Vegas to Utah. Vertex assigned me a case manager and promised they would send the information to my insurance.

He squeezed my hand, bringing me back to reality. "What are you thinking?" he asked, with his goofy smile and wide, bright eyes. We heard an animal off in the distance and turned our faces to the right, just in time for the third shooting star.

"I once heard that a shooting star is bad to wish on," I started. "Because we are wishing on something that is already dead".

He immediately interrupted with an enthusiastic tone, "Actually, that dead star carries in it all sorts of bacteria and cells and other scientific stuff that is the perfect culmination to create new life, it just needs to land in the right environment."

I thought back to the day my dad had to rent a wheelchair and push me around Six Flags on a family vacation. It hurt my lungs too much to walk. I hated inconveniencing everybody just to stop and take "breathing breaks". Maybe soon I will be in the right environment. Maybe my lungs are that perfect combination of bacteria, cells, and scientific stuff waiting for the right environment to thrive. My third wish was that he was right.

He kissed my forehead. Marilyn Monroe once said, "The real lover is a man who can thrill you by kissing your forehead or smiling into your eyes or just staring into space." I smiled and turned towards him as shooting star number four lit up our little world. My fourth wish was for my heart, not my lungs.

It was just after 3 a.m. and we decided to climb off the roof and go inside. Just as I stood up, I saw the final shooting star streak across the Northwest, joyously dancing, as if it was a message from the heavens sent to tell me that my life is worth living and everything I could possibly imagine would come true. Now I'm not sure on how this whole wishing on a shooting star thing actually works. But I've had four amazing wishes already, so I decided to save my final wish for the future in case I ever needed it.

When I returned from my week long road trip, a local San Diego news station (KPBS) interviewed me about athleticism, Cystic Fibrosis, and the hope Vertex gave me. The reporter asked, "Have you thought about what happens if you are denied the drug because of cost?"

The answer was "Yes". In fact, I had thought about being denied several times. But I have spent a lifetime overcoming obstacles. Each time, I have found my greatest strength in the midst of insurmountable weakness. However, what I haven't thought about was how I would tell my daddy that some pharmaceutical company just denied me the lifesaving drug that I mentioned two years ago while he was pushing me around Six Flags in a wheelchair. But then again, a drug company can't really do that. An insurance company can't really put a price on my life. Can they? Will they?

I left the interview and checked my voicemails. "Hi Klyn, this is Chris, from Vertex..." the message began. What followed was a 42 second scripted speech.

I was denied. Somewhere an executive decided my life is not worth the cost of Orkambi. Little do they know, I still have my fifth wish. And I know this great spot in Utah if I need more...

> *"Winning is not a sometime thing; it's an all the time thing. You don't win once in a while; you don't do things right once in a while; you do them right all of the time. Winning is a habit. Unfortunately, so is losing."*

> *"There is no room for second place. There is only one place in my game, and that's first place. I have finished second twice in my time at Green Bay, and I don't ever want to finish second again. There is a second place bowl game, but it is a game for losers played by losers. It is and always has been an American zeal to be first in anything we do, and to win, and to win, and to win."* - *Coach Vincent T. Lombardi*

## The Myth of Failure

There are a lot of myths today about what failure is. What does it look like? How do you decide when to quit a failing endeavor and move on versus stick the course? In today's fast-paced, instant-gratification society, we are preconditioned to believe everything happens immediately. It's easy to think that success is easy to obtain, fairly straight forward, with limited setbacks. We think that the people worth billions today were born into a life of luxury with silver spoons in their mouths and if we weren't born into the same life, we can't be uber-wealthy too.

In reality, many of today's most successful and recognizable people have had to endure failure. For example, one famous NBA star once said, "I've missed more than 9,000 shots in my career. I've lost almost 300 games. Twenty-six times, I've been entrusted to take the game winning shot and missed." If you were looking at these particular statistics on this player, you might agree with most people and expect this athlete had a very short career. You may even begin to wonder what team could ever possibly want him. However, Michael Jordan goes on to say, "I've failed over and over and over again in my life, and that is why I succeed."

Living with her grandmother in a home without electricity, running water, or plumbing, Oprah was taught to recite the bible at an early age. The people closest to her dreamt that one day, she would grow up to be a maid for a white family that might "treat her with respect". She was sexually abused, physically abused, and raped repeatedly. As if that wasn't traumatic enough, she gave birth to a boy when she was only 14 years old. The boy died as an infant.

When she moved in with her father, he taught her the importance of reading books; making it a requirement to read weekly and create a book report based off that week's reading. After high school, Oprah received a scholarship to Tennessee State University.

When she was 22 years old, her life finally looked like it was going to change for the better. She landed a job as a news anchor and her dreams were coming true. Unfortunately, soon after that she was fired for being too "dull".

"Rock bottom became the solid foundation for which I built my life." J.K. Rowling was rejected 12 times by publishers for her work, *Harry Potter and the Sorcerer's Stone*. In fact, she used to refer to herself as the biggest failure she knew.

What makes some people rise up against adversity to eventually be a Five-Time NBA MVP instead of quitting the sport? How does Oprah create the OWN television network when she should have had a mile-long list of excuses? What mindset did J.K. Rowling have when she sent her work off to yet another publisher, but eventually led her to a net worth just over $1 billion?

The truth is every highly successful entrepreneur and athlete failed their way to success. Read that again. Every successful person you have ever met, read about, watched a documentary on, and strived to emulate... failed their way to success. Failure needs to be seen as an event, not a person. When you fail, and you will, emotionally distance yourself from the situation. Take a logical look at the events that unfolded and what hidden golden nuggets can come from them. There is always a silver lining. There is always something that can be learned and then, can be reapplied in another variation towards your end goal. Failure is not definite. Winston Churchill famously said, "Success is going from failure to failure without the loss of enthusiasm."

Andre' Phillipe van den Broeck was a great kid in high school. He was the poster child for how right things could go. He received straight A's and was captain of the soccer team. "I wanted to play professionally, so after graduation, I started training with a Dallas professional team. Then I went to Virginia for one year to play D1 Soccer. Unfortunately, I had to leave mid-season to be with my mom during my parent's divorce."

"I used to be a really good kid, but for 3-4 years I completely lashed out. I hung out with the wrong crowd, did drugs, sold drugs and got into a lot of fights. I lived a very charmed life up until that point. Growing up, we weren't wealthy, we did okay. However, seeing my parents' 25 years of marriage end made me change from the guy everybody liked to the guy nobody knew."

"I was really ashamed of that story because my parents raised me better than that, and I'm a believer. I am a Christian and I realized that it's just part of my testimony now. Instead of being ashamed and fearful of it, I want people to understand you have to learn to live with consequences of your decisions, but you don't have to let it define you (if you don't want to). I was getting back on track. I grew a lot from it and it was a time of the most growth that I've ever experienced. "

"Now I'm thankful for it. At my most pivotal point, I was either going to spend my life in jail or end up dead. It's not about what happened, but more about where I came from. I certainly don't deserve what I have now."

The years after high school weren't the only tough times of his life. He had a considerable amount of adversity with his first company too. After getting his life back on track, by 2008 he was 27 and owned a real estate company. Times were lucrative for him. "It was a unique business model and I was practically printing money... I started doing most of the work from my boat and it was really the first time I'd ever pulled in a few hundred thousand a year. I had a partner, and we were expanding to four offices." They knew it was time to take their business to the next level and multiply their revenue. However, then came the real estate crash. "The market and I tanked along with it, as foolish as I was with money. I came home to an eviction notice on my door, my cars repossessed, my dog was out of food and I had no idea how I was going to feed him. My lights were turned off." However, Andre' didn't give up. After closing up his real estate company, he started over and eventually formed his highly successful menswear company, Andre' Phillipe Inc.

Blake Cavignac, founder of YoungPro Elite stated, "Never let other people's perceptions of failures or rejections keep you down. It comes down to conditioning your mind. The most successful people have a different view of failure vs. success. They do the right things and when they know they have a great idea, they don't let anything or anyone stop them from achieving it. It may not happen as originally planned, but that's okay. Successful people keep going, keep tweaking, and they keep figuring it out. They have an outcome in mind and at some point, success versus failure it isn't even up for the conversation. The success part is inevitable. Success will happen."

Growing up, motivational speaker and author, Cameron Morrissey, was taught that in order to be successful, he needed to join a business program in a major university after high school. "You're supposed to be hired by some Fortune 500 company right out of the gate, yet nobody tells you that only 15-20% of the students get that opportunity. My initial failure was realizing I didn't have a job lined up, nor was I going to because of the competitive nature. I wasn't in the top 5% of my class, so I had to move back in with my parents and tell them that my part-time college job was now going to be my full-time career." It was a rough start for somebody who now communicates daily with over a million social media subscribers, is the author of three books that have been published in 30 countries, and is a highly sought-after business speaker.

Don Langmo, founder of Healthcare Support and Healthcare Scouts, opens up about his biggest failure, "I was kind of implored about the idea of creating a recruiting firm based on placing a niche type of physician. When we place nurses, we make $8,000; when we place physicians, it's around $20,000. So I thought I had a great idea. Since the money was good, let's create a company revolved around exclusively placing a certain type of physician in their perfectly suited job. I picked MD psychiatrists because they are fun people and it would be a great business. But we never had a single placement. Not one. This was as big of a failure as you could ever imagine. At the time, I put $200,000 into it, which was six months' profit from my other company. It was a big deal. I was certain it would work so I kept working harder and harder. Even though it eventually failed, I still keep that business card framed near my desk as a reminder that you're never as smart as you think you are. Even with all of these brilliant ideas that you can conjure up, things don't always work the way you choose. But it's not end of the world. It taught me that healthcare was a good industry, and now we're doing really well because of the lessons I learned."

"Success is about believing in yourself. If you keep working hard, you'll eventually find a way." Langmo, studies biographies and history in his spare time and shares, "In my mind, business is the only exciting adventure that's left. You can't explore new places anymore. Business is the last frontier where you can create something from nothing. There are no boundaries. You can build something new and different, that the world hasn't discovered yet." His company is growing quickly and is currently valued at over $75 million.

*"Your past is meant to guide you, not define you."* - *Anonymous*

*"Go and do it, try to learn from it. You'll fail at something but that's a learning experience. You need to take that on to the next experience."* - *Pierre Omidyar, Founder of eBay*

*"You're going to make tons of mistakes. There are things every year in Facebook's existence that could have killed us, but you bounce back and you learn."* - *Mark Zuckerberg, Founder of Facebook*

In every decision you make, define the worst-case scenario you can imagine happening. Take a hard look at what you could learn from that failure, should it come to pass. Then, after you have come to terms with what you've discovered, you can start to make your decision. Is there the potential to learn more from the failure than you are risking? As the examples above clearly demonstrate, you can bounce back from anything.

Chapter 2

# The Power of Transformation

The way the most influential people view failure is partly what makes them influential. In *Eat, Pray, Love* Elizabeth Gilbert shares, "We all want things to stay the same. Settle for living in misery because we're afraid of change, of things crumbling to ruins. Then I looked around to this place (referring to the Mausoleum of Augustus in Rome), at the chaos it has endured – the way it has been adapted, burned, pillaged and found a way to build itself back up again. And I was reassured, maybe my life hasn't been so chaotic, it's just the world that is, and the real trap is getting attached to any of it. Ruin is a gift. Ruin is the road to transformation."

You see, this red mark on my chest, these scars on my abs, these sores on the corners of my mouth, all show to the world my battle with the #1 genetic killer in the United States. When I was born, my life expectancy was only 14 years. If born today with my variation of the disease, you could expect to live approximately 37 years. So at 26 years old, my life is 70% over. Every few months since I was 16, I was hospitalized and put on IV therapy. When my veins could no longer support a lifetime of IV's, I underwent a surgery to install my port. This small, red device sits just under my skin on my chest, and feeds up through my jugular and into my heart, allowing for easier blood draw and easier administration for IV fluids and antibiotics. Although hardly noticeable to other people, I still think about it every time I wear a low cut dress. I have spent more birthdays and holidays in the hospital, than I have at home with my family.

The mucous in my lungs is abnormally sticky and prone to infection due to an imbalance of sodium chloride passing through the epithelial cells. Once an infection begins, in a matter of mere weeks, I go from running at the gym to coughing up blood and needing oxygen. Then, I claw my way back through vigorous physical therapy, hours of nebulizing medications, countless pills, and forcing my body to hack out the infection. Any day now, an infection could begin again. And with every infection my chances of rebounding diminish due to antibiotic resistance.

Despite this, I landed my dream career as a recruiter. I thrived on reaching out to people who had no idea who I was, building instant rapport with them, and using our combined strengths as leverage for our individual goals. Then we used these individual goals to create a lasting legacy that made the world a better place. Through that job, I discovered not only do I love people, but I love bringing people together.

Recruiting is a skill that came very natural to me. Growing up, my father moved us around the country following his extensive sales career. Because of this, I've had more jobs than I've had years on this planet. Acing interviews became second nature for me. With all of that practice, I was naturally ready to start teaching other people how to market themselves to get their dream career.

My first day as a "real headhunter", the team was welcoming and I was eagerly ready to utilize my track record of success to get more candidates, more careers, in the most efficient way. I loved the rush of the cold calls, and my IV pole became a normal office staple in much the same way as half-full company coffee cups on everyone's desk at 9 am. Unfortunately, about two months into every new job the first hospitalization takes place. But this time when it happened I was both humbled and overwhelmed by the number of flowers, texts, and calls I received. The entire company was more than accepting of my "condition" and willing to overlook my two weeks off despite my short time on their payroll.

By hospitalizations two through six I can tell that human resources is starting to realize the amount of revenue I bring in doesn't quite break even for the weeks I am in the hospital and not working. They rationalize keeping me on board because, "It's Klyn, she's a top producer...when she's here. She'll bounce back." The coworkers start to get annoyed they can't take as much time off as I can and they have to cover a few urgent matters while I am out.

It is at this point that somebody does what I was hoping they wouldn't do ever since my warm welcome. They look at the data and somehow I'm let go. They always find a good reason, whether it's suddenly performance based or that my department is restructuring. As usual, the entire executive team feels a type of guilt. They say, "we really like you on board so we will write any recommendation letter you want." And because this process is all too familiar, I begin again. No insurance, no income, but a track record of success to get a corner office at my next gig. Plus, now I have yet another impressively worded recommendation letter to take to the next place that will fire me in roughly 9-12 months.

I sold my house and headed to San Diego in April 2013; partially after another let-go from a recruiting firm, partially after an ex-boyfriend wanted to rekindle. Shortly after moving in with him, I landed a position as an associate director of a biotech and pharmaceutical recruiting firm. By the second month, we rearranged the house to make room for all of my medical equipment since I was being put on 24-7 IV antibiotic therapy.

There was no way to hide the progression of the disease. The nebulizers I did for two hours a day were raucous. I spent hours wearing a vest that forced my lungs to cough, and it became difficult for him to watch. My IV pole became a coat rack on the weeks I wasn't required to use it, looming over us like an unstated fate. My cough would wake him up at night and I lost 15 pounds due to stress and antibiotics. Finishing the course of IV antibiotics, his sister pulled me aside and said, "We love you, but he told me he never wants to be married."

There I was, 1,500 miles away from friends or family with a heart shattered into pieces.

I had nowhere to live, I was single, and I needed an oxygen tank for the first time in my life. Luckily, my employer was tolerant of my medical absences and after the second hospitalization, I threw myself into my work. I was terrified I would be fired if I took any more time off.

I spent a few nights in my car until my dad found a family friend three hours away from San Diego that agreed to take me in until I found a stable home. I was up early and fell asleep late. I slowly and foolishly stopped creating time for my treatments to instead focus on generating enough income to pay down the last hospital bill. Then after an exhaustive day, my boss called to inform me if I didn't move to San Diego immediately, they would need to replace me. I scraped everything together and moved that night to an entirely unaffordable place, thereby at least saving my career.

Driving my car through the mountains that night, I heard a rattle in the engine. The moments before your car breaks down, everything goes in slow motion. Time really is relative. You know what is happening under the hood, but you don't have the time to react. It reminded me of how my lungs tremble right before a violent cough. There's a tickle, which I ignore.

Unfortunately, the subtle hum of the engine told me something just wasn't right. I focused on driving forward, relishing in the way the roads curve around the unforgiving landscape. The soft hum got louder, turning into a rattle. I exhaled and heard the pockets of phlegm get caught in my chest as it attempted to escape my lungs. I heard the engine shaking the car before I felt what's next. Then, the violent, all consuming cough shut me down. At that same moment, as if some secret synchronicity was at play, my car broke down too. Scared and alone, catching my breath...I assessed the situation and knew that both my car and I were ready for a tune up. Except this time, maybe one of us won't ever return to the road.

Even though I saw the blood on my shirt from my latest coughing fit, I made the decision that I should put off hospitalization #3. I was scared, but I couldn't request more time off. I thought to myself "I am one call away from not being able to afford my new place and losing my career".

How many of you have been there? When you find yourself in that one moment when you know you can make a great impression to your team if you just stay in the office a little longer. When you think to yourself that if you just miss one of your kid's events, you can fill your calendar with important meetings that can shape your career. When you wonder if you stay just an extra hour, will your spouse mind?

Just one cold call away from my dreams, I start struggling to walk from the parking lot to the office. My tongue always tasted like blood. I knew I had to give in, so I begrudgingly held my head down and called my boss. "I need to go back on IV's". My lung function was at 47%.

Checking in to the ER, a good friend and attorney called and asked "What are you really working for?" The truth is, I didn't know. I worked because I loved recruiting. I worked because that's what successful women do. Men don't marry women who aren't in charge of their careers. My bosses are great and I want to impress them. Answer after answer seemed inadequate and I realized the answer was the same answer senator Paul Tsongas stated when he decided to not run for reelection after being diagnosed with cancer. "No man ever said on his deathbed, I wish I had spent more time in the office."

My friend stated with grave concern, "Klyn, I don't want the next time I talk to you to be about how to draft your will." Three days later, I quit my career despite the fear of burning bridges with two powerful CEOs. To this day, neither has spoken to me.

And here I am, speaking to you, in a world with endless possibilities, about how according to Elizabeth Gilbert in *Eat, Pray, Love*, "Ruin is the road to transformation." Because I woke up one morning with the epiphany that life is too short, regardless of if I lived 26 years or 100 years, I needed to spend every day smiling and laughing.

I wasn't given a life expectancy that allowed me to know that I still have tomorrow to get things done. Instead I was given the opportunity to chase the life I really was meant to live. My life is short, but so is yours.

None of us have the luxury of a guarantee that we will make it into the office tomorrow. It's not the income, it's not the cars, and it's not the brand names filling our closet. We are alive for a bigger purpose. Once we truly hit our rock bottoms, we can begin to see what the top of our mountains can look like, and the road we need to take to get there.

It is equally important to remember what author and motivational speaker Zig Ziglar said, "...failure is an event and not a person." The most successful people do not take failure personally. They take it as an indication that there is room for improvement, and as a direction showing them where they should focus energy to improve.

Steve Mehr, millionaire and founder of WebShark 360, states, "to get through adversity, you must emotionally distance yourself from the situation to see the failure and what actually happened." Imagine you are a third party to the situation, and it becomes much easier to take the emotion out of it. "Look at the facts. Look at what is known and what should be known for next time."

*"I'm thankful for my struggle because without it I wouldn't have stumbled across my strength." - Alex Elle, author*

*"I'd say not to judge the challenges that happen in business as initially bad. Often, those 'bad things' turn out to be good! Right before a breakthrough, it can feel a lot like a breakdown." - Jeff Shelton, Entrepreneur*

25

> *"Winners are not afraid of losing. But losers are. Failure is part of the process of success. People who avoid failure also avoid success." - Robert T. Kiyosaki,*
>
> *"It's failure that gives you the proper perspective on success." - Ellen DeGeneres, TV Personality*
>
> *"Everything in your life worth having, is uphill" - Dr. John Maxwell, author*

"Success is a lousy teacher. It seduces smart people into thinking they can't lose," Bill Gates wrote in his book *The Road Ahead.* "Today's can't-fail product could wind up obsolete tomorrow, which could be what's happening to desktop personal computers and the Windows operating system that often runs them." Sure, anybody will find success more enjoyable than adversity, but it is the failure that teaches the most and gives you the best opportunity for growth.

In fact, living in fear of failure will hold you back from ever becoming a millionaire, from ever achieving your goals. Successful people are not afraid to step outside their comfort zones, to expand their comfort level. They do not view a failure as definite. They do not view it as a final result, signifying that you must quit. They take the risks because they know failure will happen and it is a learning experience. It is a chance to create a variation.

Don Langmo, founder of a national healthcare recruiting firm states, "I think that most entrepreneurs if not all, really relish the challenge. They don't want it to be easy, they want a battle. They want to fight; they want to compete. Just like in sports, you've never met an athlete that won every game. There is no such thing as a real athlete that has never lost. The losses make the victory sweeter. Business is no different, it's a sport. It's a group of people playing by a set of rules trying to beat another group of people assembled by a different coach. My job as CEO is to build a winning team and create a situation where they all work well together. If we have a better team than the other people, then more often than not, we will win. I love competition. Entrepreneurs love competition; it appeals to us more than anything."

Jeff Shelton, founder and owner of San Diego based Wholesale Warranties, states, "In dealing with adversity, you don't think about all of the things going wrong. You see your goal and you just go. You have to keep a clear vision and know everything else is a distraction." Shelton knows in his mind, what he needs to do in the week ahead and works tirelessly until everything is completed.

> *"Our greatest weakness lies in giving up. The most certain way to succeed is always to try just one more time." - Thomas Edison, inventor*

Former NFL quarterback and Sports Commentator Boomer Esiason wasn't raised in a lap of luxury. In a very candid interview he shares, "I think a lot is dependent upon the environment in which you grow up. I never had a mom or female influence in my life, as a child. Growing up like that, day in and day out, hardens you." Esiason was a street kid. His childhood taught him how to figure problems out on his own in order to get things accomplished because he had nobody to fall back on. "My father was the most interesting and greatest man of my life. He was a part of the greatest generation born during the great depression. He grew up sacrificing for his family and his country. He enlisted into World War II. After experiencing horrendous moments in war, he returned and tried to raise a family. When I was seven, my dad lost the love of his life. He was in his mid-forties and raised three kids on his own (without public subsidies). There was no time for sorrow or negativity. I never heard my dad complain about war, losing his wife, or anything." Esiason's philosophy on life came from watching his father's indelible spirit and it was that spirit that got him through what he considers one of his biggest failures.

The way you react to a failure, the adaptation you choose to focus on, ultimately propels you forward or holds you back depending on the way you look at it. "After high school, I had one college scholarship offer to play football. Some thought, 'wow that is a success', yet others swore 'I must not have been that good'. In high school, people thought I was the man; everyone knew my name, I won all the games, everybody loved me. The cold reality was, now I was the 11th string quarterback. I remembered thinking, 'how am I 11th on the list?" There's a level of failure associated any time somebody goes from the absolute top of their game, being the big fish in a relatively small pond, to now being a small fish in a much grander pond. "I could have given in and quit, but those moments never entered my mind. I never thought of quitting. I knew there's going to be a mountain to climb but I also knew it wouldn't be impossible. The message resonates with me still today, at age 54, you can never allow a dream to die and my dream was to be a professional football player. I was motivated by the fear of failure and by many people in my life who surrounded me and never thought I could accomplish my dream." The obstacles in your life are meant to guide you. They are not meant to define you.

Rob LaBreche was a co-founder and President of a booming financial services company in San Diego. In just under five years, his company grew from 3 to 700 employees. That is, until 2007 when the financial industry fell apart. Literally one day after his wedding, he walked into his office, where a huge banner reading, "Congratulations!" was displayed. Seconds later, a call from the CEO came in. He answered it, expecting to hear an enthusiastic tone. Instead he was shocked to find out that he was fired. Not only that, but the sales, marketing, and public relations departments he was in charge of were being let go as well. "It took a little bit of time to digest the situation. It was mentally devastating. But I realized how fortunate I was, how it was an opportunity."

He went home to his new bride and declared, "I want to start a company to help people with financial literacy. In order to do that, we have to spend every dime we have to make it happen. She teared up." Deep down, he needed some time to evaluate losing his career and what this meant for the future he was trying to build with his wife but his situation didn't afford him that luxury.

The next morning, they woke up and she said "I wouldn't have it any other way, we need to start that company but we need to do it for you, for us, and for everyone". Together, they took perhaps the biggest initial failure of his life, which occurred in the absolute worst time, and treated it as a stepping stone to build the life that was waiting. "It's about layers of success. I've learned over the years my definition has really changed. I want to be happy and have the people around me happy. I've discovered (partly through the adversity) that I am very passionate about financial wellness, and I now can teach hundreds of thousands of people across the country how to better improve their finances." Rob LeBreche is a shining example that obstacles are simply stepping stones. After that momentous day, he went on to form iGrad, a financial education company focused on improving financial literacy for college students. Since launching, his literacy platforms have served over 200 campuses and 1,000,000 students; making it one of the most widely used financial literacy platforms available. It is not the load that breaks you; it is how you carry it.

> *"You'll face complex financial problems, decision-based dilemmas, long hours, sudden changes, and predictions that egregiously fail. You must remember that all these challenges, while difficult to face, are a natural part of being an entrepreneur. Success in business ownership is rarely a matter of how many challenges you face so much as it is a matter of how you face those challenges." - Jayson Demers, founder and CEO of Audience Bloom*

When you set a goal, whether it is to start a company or become a professional football player, you must be ready for challenges. You must be ready for adversity. You must be ready to learn from setbacks and turn them into comebacks. For everything that could possibly go wrong when you start a company (financial problems, long hours, unpredictability, employee turnover, rising competition) there are just as many things that could go right. Stay focused and remember that all challenges come with the territory. Jeff Shelton, owner of one of the fastest growing private companies in San Diego shares, "it's not about how many problems you face, it's about your attitude in facing those problems."

Beth Sufian is a beacon of hope and inspiration to many Cystic Fibrosis patients. She is in her fifties and thriving despite her disease. In a very heartfelt interview she chronicles one of her biggest challenges, one that ultimately was a turning point in her life. "In 1993, I was working at a big law firm and one of the local Cystic Fibrosis doctors asked me if I would help a child-patient get Social Security benefits because the family had tried for two years to obtain benefits with no success."

At the time, Sufian was a lawyer but wasn't practicing disability law so was concerned she could not help the boy. However, Beth's own Cystic Fibrosis physician, Dr. John Jacoby, knew there was something about Beth's work ethic and passion for helping others that couldn't be ignored. He told her she should try to help the boy otherwise he may never receive the benefits he desperately needed to pay for life saving medical care. Beth told the family she would help and not charge a fee. It took many hours of work, but Beth succeeded in her first case in this field.

Meanwhile, it was clear Sufian's job at the big law firm was not good for her health. The firm found out she had cystic fibrosis and she was afraid she would be fired. She had heard from many others with Cystic Fibrosis who were fired once their employer's found out they had the condition. Dr. Jacoby encouraged her to find a new path to a successful career. "You're getting sick working all the time, and you find the work you are doing pro bono for people with CF to be so meaningful." Beth decided to start her own law firm. Dr. Jacoby started giving Beth's contact information to other patients and a law firm focusing on the rights of people with disabilities was born.

Her purpose was to help people with disabilities

obtain the benefits they need to live a higher quality of life and to obtain insurance coverage for necessary treatment. Initially, patients with Cystic Fibrosis dominated her caseload. The first two years she worked early mornings and late nights without significant income. In 1998, she created a legal hotline to answer legal questions for those in the CF community.

As traction grew, Sufian gained a new client, American Biosystems, a privately held company that made a medical device for cystic fibrosis patients. This wearable device vibrates their lungs which makes it easier to cough out the thick mucous that clogs the airways of people with Cystic Fibrosis. If patients are able to cough out bacteria-ridden secretions, they live longer. The equipment was revolutionizing in terms of treatments for patients, however insurance companies refused to pay for this life-altering machine.

The battle to obtain insurance coverage for the device took six years and legal actions in 12 states, but Sufian and her law partner prevailed. Through their efforts she was able to extend the life expectancy of patients with Cystic Fibrosis. In fact, as I write this my American Biosystems vest is sitting in the corner of my office. Looking back, I can reflect on just how life-saving her work was to me and many in the CF community. Nowadays, this equipment is easily covered and thousands of patients can live longer and stronger lives.

Beth Sufian says, "I always remind myself very quickly (in moments of failure) that I've had a very good life and am very lucky to have a very good family, friends and a career I love. There are many people who are not so lucky. If I feel discouraged, I remind myself that I am thankful for everything I have accomplished and for the ability to help others that are not so fortunate."

Sufian chooses to see the positive in her life as a way to get her through the negative. She is far from alone. In moments of adversity, most successful people focus their energy on what they already have rather than what they don't have or didn't achieve immediately. To date, she has helped over 45,000 patients and families through her legal hotline and legal advocacy. Sufian's efforts continue to provide a higher quality of life to countless people.

Chances are, if you picked up this book, and are dedicating your time to reading it, you clearly have some skills, tools, and resources that are already in place to set your future on the right track. Many people would rather concern their free time with reality television, trivial pursuits of fleeting happiness, and short-term gratification. It was once said, most people stop living at 25 years old and die in their 80's. The quality of life becomes repetitive and they cease to seek out what they want, letting fear or the lack of an ability to make a decision, be the ticket to their own demise. Darren Hardy, publisher of SUCCESS magazine, once said, "We don't get burned out by what we do, only when we forget why we are doing it."

## Know Your Why

*"Do what you're passionate about." - Jeff Bezos, CEO Amazon*

*"Discover your uniqueness and learn to exploit it in the service of others, and you are guaranteed success,*

*happiness, and prosperity." - Larry Winget, best-selling author*

When asked why he wanted to start YoungPro Elite, Blake Cavignac explained "it was born out of my frustration." Although Cavignac was fortunate in life to have his parents pay for his education, he never went to class. "My teachers weren't ever something I wanted to be like. I believe that you can learn something from everyone, but I didn't want to spend my time with them." What he did want to spend time doing was working as a real estate investor and learning more about business from people who are creating tomorrows. "I started YoungPro Elite because I truly believe most of the lessons they teach you in the traditional education system offer absolutely nothing in terms of support for a successful career. Our focus is to partner with CEO's and executives with the intent on helping them learn about young professionals. We focus on how to maximize young talent, set them up for success, and positively impact the economy simultaneously. It impacts the world, if you have cohesive communication."

Entrepreneur consultant J.D. Davids shares the mindset that has helped him build, grow, and monetize innovative startup companies since 1991. "I didn't have money for college, so I spent four years' active duty in the Marine Corps. Through that, I learned a few things. First, that you can do a lot more than you are capable of if you're pushed. Our self-limitations are only what holds us back. As a result, you have to have resilience and determination to never give up, while keeping your eye on the prize. As an entrepreneur, you have to overcome obstacles. You will have good and bad days. You have to be in it for a bigger purpose than money, sailboats, and islands. You need to have a desire to help your customers solve problems. If that's your driver, you will be successful. If your motives are right, you'll get through the bad days."

"There are a ton of entrepreneurs out there with fantastic ideas who are good at building a product, but they can't understand navigating the waters when the business grows from three people in a garage, to raising their first $20,000 to $100,000 to $1 million. Scaling up has an infinite number of potholes. I like to be the person that comes in and navigates that water, because I've done it twenty times. In entrepreneurship, if you want to be successful in any industry (commerce, fitness, events, technology, widgets), find somebody who has done what you want to do and get them on your advisory board. It's about having people at the table who have been there and have successfully done what you want to do." As a direct result of his personal enjoyment and passion for helping entrepreneurs learn how to sail choppy waters, he has been able to raise over a billion dollars in start-up capital.

Davids' believes that people need to break free from the negative thinking that holds them back from truly living life. "Take the gifts you've been given, and then maximize them. Many times, negative thinking is simply fear, perfectionism, self-criticism, and shame." If you know your purpose, then when waters get choppy, you can still sail around the world.

Anyone who has read the book "Between A Rock and A Hard Place" or seen the movie "127 Hours" is familiar with Aron Ralston. In 2003, his right arm was trapped between a canyon wall and a dislodged boulder off a remote cliff in Utah. Excruciating pain riddled his body, he was out of water, out of food, and he was forced to contemplate the reality he may never see his loved ones again.

Knowing he would soon die, for 120 long hours, he had flashbacks of everything in life he loved. Thoughts of his family, his career, his love for canyoneering, and premonitions of his son and future wife filled his head. In the depths of despair, he knew if he didn't make a life-altering decision, his body would be discovered lifeless, perhaps years from now, perhaps never. He mentally clung to his flashbacks and wishes, and decided to grasp a dull knife in one hand and use it to cut off his other arm.

Four hours away from that same canyon is where I had that magical night making wishes on shooting stars while wrapped in the arms of a man that I was falling for faster than the stars were falling from the sky. I was mentally preparing for whatever life I could live, even if it is dramatically shortened because my insurance can't justify the $259,000 per-year cost of Orkambi. In my heart, when all seems lost, I make wishes.

I have made wishes for Orkambi to show up on my door step and breathe new hope into my failing lungs, to have an alarm clock instead of an alarm cough. I have made wishes to collect more moments instead of things; like visiting New York this New Year's eve with my best friend. I have made wishes that I can create a company focused on talent acquisition strategies and implementation for high-growth companies. I have made wishes that my parents can go to sleep at night without the constant worry that the next day they will be notified of my declining health.

Lastly, I wished that one day when I'm gray haired and surrounded by friends and family, I'll be sitting on a chair and someone's child will say, "Klyn, what was your first real love like?" and I won't have to reach into my memory for a description. I'll just point across the room and say "that's him".

Pneumonia. six weeks after our RV trip, I checked myself into the hospital with a 39% lung function. So far, the IV combination of antibiotics to treat this latest infection wasn't working. Even if the insurance companies reverse their decision, I was now technically too sick to be approved for Orkambi.

Intestinal blockage. I hadn't eaten solid food for four days. The same man who held me on the rooftop is now holding me in a hospital bed listening to the surgeon say "She will need surgery if the Nasogastric tube doesn't work. It isn't a matter of if; it is a matter of when. I suggest you get ready. At this point, her bowels will explode inside her stomach. It's a matter of hours."

Five times they tried to jam a plastic pipe into my nose to reach my stomach and siphon out the food I enjoyed over the past week. Five times they ripped apart my nasal cavity. Blood shot out my nose and mouth, gagged my throat, and high dosage narcotics were flushed through my port in an attempt to sedate me. Pain shot through my body - excruciating, life-altering, mind-numbing pain.

I can't imagine what Aron went through as he jammed the dull blade into his own forearm, watching in a surreal state the way his blood pooled and danced down the side of the cold, dark canyon. I stopped thinking about Aron long enough to feel my own blood pool and dance down the back of my throat.

Aron survived. He hacked off the last bit of flesh while clinging to his "why" and stumbled off away from his arm. His reason to live was that powerful.

I knew I was losing a part of my lungs to

pneumonia. I looked back at what life was like a mere six weeks ago, when a man kissed my forehead and made a wish that we could find a way to let all of our heartache and heartbreak from the past guide us towards an optimistic future.

Henry Ford once said, "Whether you think you can or think you can't, you're right". I know I will survive this because my wishes and my 'why's' are stronger than anything Cystic Fibrosis has. I will leave a bit of my lungs to the world just as Aron left his arm in the canyon, and continue to fulfill my wishes with what tools my body is giving me to work with. I will visit New York with my best friend. I will spend many Christmases with my family in Texas. I will create a recruiting company that helps entrepreneurial focused companies. I will build a life with a man who looks at me and thinks, "that's her" the same way I look at him.

> *"In the end, we only regret the chances we didn't take, relationships we were too afraid to have, and the decisions we waited too long to make."* - Lewis Carroll, author
>
> *"If you fell down yesterday, stand up today."* - H.G. Wells, author
>
> *"If you're afraid to fail, you're probably going to fail."* - Kobe Bryant, NBA hall of famer

Never before in history, have things been able to change so rapidly. You are moments away from any given breakthrough; you can send a tweet to a celebrity and be on national news the very next day. There are an infinite number of opportunities accessible via the smart phone which is probably less than 20 feet from you at this moment. Somehow, in the world of possibilities, something will guide you. Your purpose in this life is available to you right now. You have to know what it is. When you find your passion, you also find your first glimpse of success.

*"If you don't love what you're doing failure is pretty much guaranteed." - Biz Stone, Founder of Twitter*

*"Why do you get out of bed every morning and why should the world care? If you don't know why you do what you do and people respond, how will you ever get people to vote for you or buy from you or more importantly, be loyal?" - Simon Sinek, author*

*"If you never try for things, you'll never know and that's the real failure." - Anonymous*

Chapter 3

# The Power of a Decision

We all have regrets in life, things we settled for because we were afraid to make a change. Decisions we shied away from because we were never sure the timing was right, the money was there, or we were as prepared as we wanted to be to make the leap. As I look back on my life, the decision to drop out of college isn't one that I regret.

Winters in Iowa are particularly harsh. With wind chills dipping below zero degrees and an average snowfall of eight inches, trekking to campus with a backpack full of books to avoid driving on icy roads is an essential way of life. If you want that slip of paper in four years that proves you are an accomplished member of academia, you find a will in your heart to make it happen.

At the time, I lived roughly three miles from the heart of Iowa State, in an apartment that I shared with a friend from high school. She was studying nutrition; I was studying business. We spent many nights discussing everything from branch chain amino acids, to the hot guys, to the professors we loved to hate.

Every morning at 5 a.m. I would wake up, rush to complete my hour long treatments, and then put on several layers of clothes to hike through the snowfall to the nearest bus stop. Once there, I would wait patiently in the cold for what seemed like hours as the subzero temperatures stung my nostrils and agitated my lungs.

After a 20 minute bus ride, I would trek across campus to the first class of the day. As my airways adjusted from the freezing cold to the incinerating heat from the classrooms, my lungs would become agitated. Rather than cough in the crowded atmosphere of a first year lecture hall, I would opt to sneak around the corner and cough in the privacy of an empty hallway. I was late to almost every class. By the time my lungs cleared and I felt comfortable entering the room, I would open the heavy doors and quickly walk to one of the only few seats left in the room; the whole time under the silent, judgmental glare of the students and professors.

A 25-pound backpack added to the pain in my lungs as I carried it across campus for miles every day. I would sit outside again in the blizzard, waiting patiently for the bus, ready to go home and complete another hour of nebulized therapies. Finally, by 7 p.m., I could start really studying for the next day's exams.

I remembered thinking, why am I doing this? With my life expectancy, was I really living life to the fullest? Were freezing temperatures and angry professors really the route I wanted my life to take? Would I live long enough to pay off this massive burden of debt?

It didn't matter how I phrased my questions to myself. I tried to convince myself that getting the degree could prove to the CF community that anything is possible. I tried to the best of my ability, over and over, to justify that what I was doing was worth it in the long run. However, over time I started to realize that the reality for myself was that there could be no long run, and maybe a business degree wasn't really for me.

I came to Iowa State, full of hope and spirit. I received an associate's degree in general studies from Iowa Western Community College with a 4.0 cumulative GPA. I was on the leadership program, received several scholarships, and was very involved on campus as an ambassador. Like the sun, my optimism disappeared that winter. I resented academia. I resented my struggle. I resented the path my life was on.

During one of the blizzards, I sat waiting for the bus alone. After waiting for a half-hour in the cold, I received a text message on my phone alerting me the campus was closed due to inclement weather. A wave of exhaustion instantly hit me that, to this day, I can't describe. I was up at 4 a.m. that day, completed my medications, coughed due to the harboring of a severe lung infection, and had put off another round of IV antibiotics just to make it to the bus on time.

When I read that text, I immediately thought to myself, 'What if my husband attends this university? If I fall in love out here, am I stuck here? If I graduate from this college, my future job will more than likely be in a 200 mile radius. If I stay on this current trajectory in my life, my future will be based off this life, right here in Iowa.'

I was frozen. Frozen in fear, frozen in angst, frozen in time. Suddenly, I was outside of my body looking at my pitiful soul, alone on a bench waiting for a bus that would never come.

The next day I dropped out of college. That weekend I sold everything in my apartment. By the end of the month, I was driving my beat-up Camaro 1,400 miles south to Orlando, Florida with $500 to my name and the insight that if I'm going to be stuck somewhere, I want to be stuck in the happiest place on Earth.

*"If you want something you've never had, you must be willing to do something you've never done." - Thomas Jefferson, author, Brewer, and Founding Father.*

*"The hardest thing to do is start." - Jack Dorsey, Twitter*

*"Action is the real measure of intelligence." - Napoleon Hill*

The earlier you make decisions; the more time those decisions have to turn into measurable results. We all start off the same in the world, helpless. We rely on other people for basic necessities; shelter, food, water, healthcare. The human race could not survive if we were abandoned at birth. What we are exposed to and our natural tendencies, makes all the difference in who we become. Robert Frost captured this eloquently in one of his most famous poems.

*Two roads diverged in a yellow wood,*
*And sorry I could not travel both*
*And be one traveler, long I stood*
*And looked down one as far as I could*
*To where it bent in the undergrowth;*

*Then took the other, as just as fair,*
*And having perhaps the better claim*
*Because it was grassy and wanted wear,*
*Though as for that the passing there*
*Had worn them really about the same,*

*And both that morning equally lay*
*In leaves no step had trodden black.*
*Oh, I kept the first for another day!*

*Yet knowing how way leads on to way*
*I doubted if I should ever come back.*

*I shall be telling this with a sigh*
*Somewhere ages and ages hence:*
*Two roads diverged in a wood, and I,*
*I took the one less traveled by,*
*And that has made all the difference.*

-Robert Frost

In his book, *The Compound Effect*, Darren Hardy discusses the importance of choice. "In essence, you make your choices, and then your choices make you. Every decision, no matter how slight, alters the trajectory of your life: whether or not to go to college, whom to marry, to have that last drink before you drive, to indulge in gossip or stay silent, to make one more prospecting call or call it a day, to say I love you or not. Every choice has an impact on the Compound Effect of your life."

When a baby starts to walk, it is instinctual. They know they will not succeed, but they try anyway. First they stand, and they fall. They do this numerous times. Each time they look around for somebody to respond to their actions, validating if they did the right thing. When they receive encouragement (happy, enthusiastic vocal tone from a loved one or even a facial expression of recognition), they try again. The baby knows it will fall again and again, yet they stand wobbly for a bit longer each time and begin attempting to put one foot in front of the other. How is this any different from what we do every day? The baby doesn't care if it looks perfect, it isn't trying to stand sturdily and glide elegantly across the room. The way we think about success, somehow, is transformed as we age. We want to look perfect, be perfect, win awards, create highly influential and profitable companies and we believe that we have to be perfect before we can start. We believe, mistakenly, that if we aren't what we think perfection is, we won't obtain the respect we need to soar to success.

In countless studies and observations, withstanding the test of time, we can see two distinct mindsets people have as they approach a goal. The first type of person is constantly reacting to the world around them. They are a creature of circumstance. Life happens to them and they are on the defense, left wondering why things never quite go their way. They become trapped in a situation where they are too preoccupied fixing things as they happen as opposed to creating things that could happen positively for them. Negative events happen to everyone, but when multiple events are triggered, the first person is usually left picking up the pieces for the rest of their lives. Each successive event brings them deeper into their mindset of, "everything bad happens to me".

As they keep trying to dig themselves out of a metaphorical hole, it keeps getting deeper. As Will Rogers famously said, "When you find yourself in a hole, stop digging."

The second type of person is a rather elite breed. Some studies estimate that only 5% of the world's population fit into this category. These are the types of people who are in relentless pursuit of everything they want in life. As they press forward they inadvertently create the offense that the earlier type of person must instinctively be on the defense of. These people are the leaders, the visionaries, the entrepreneurs, the athletes, the achievers. These are the people who will experience failure after failure, and yet rise to the top repeatedly.

They live life in a power contained within, with external stimuli as leverage.

For example, Larry Linne is a former NFL wide receiver, best-selling author, and founder of InCite Performance Group. He has always been a sprint athlete; endurance was just not in his cards. Then in 2011 he watched one of the most elite mountain bike races in the world, the Leadville Trail 100 MTB. He made the choice to break out of his comfort zone, and attempt a feat that is tough for even trained endurance athletes.

In this event, elite athletes such as Lance Armstrong cycle over 100 miles across extreme terrain of the Colorado Rockies. Elevations start at 10,152 feet and continue to climb to 12,424 feet. Many participants have had serious medical issues; some have even given their lives to the event. Out of 2,300 bikers, only 1,200 are estimated to actually finish. "I just watched it and said to myself, I have to do this," Larry shares. He applied for a lottery ticket, knowing that if he makes it, that's his sign. They picked him.

Larry had a mere six months to train, never before even biking more than 20 miles. This is a race Lance Armstrong and elite cyclists have completed. Not former NFL wide receivers that have less than six months and no training in endurance. Knowing that the majority of people who set out to finish never do, he began to instill habits that trained his body and mind for the big day.

He physically trained, he fueled his body with proper nutrition, he read up on everything he could find that would prepare him, he watched videos, and he talked with people. He had the mindset that nothing could stop him from completing this challenge.

On his last mountain bike training ride, three weeks before the big day, he had an accident. Larry separated his shoulder, broke his collarbone and elbow, and broke three bones in his hand. The doctor sternly stated, "You're done. The pain alone will keep you from finishing this race." So what do you think Larry did? Do you think he had the realization that this accident was a sign he shouldn't complete the race? If he needed an out, the world would give him this one. Not one person could call him a quitter for not showing up that day. He had a medical recommendation not to compete in this race, not to mention he knew it would be intensely painful.

He went home. He took pain meds that night. The next morning, Linne decided to throw the medicine in the trash. He was determined to prove to himself and his family that he could overcome the pain and accomplish anything he set his mind to. He went to the toughest hill there was to climb in Colorado and climbed 3,000 feet on his bike with the philosophy, the mindset, "My legs are okay, I'm still going to train. I'm not going to give up."

On the day of the race he arrived with his arm in a sling. He had a mere 12 hours to finish to win a belt-buckle. Undeterred, he did what he had to do, not just for himself, but also to be a positive role model for his children and to be an inspiration to his wife. It took 11 hours and 24 minutes, but Larry has that belt buckle. The next year, he completed the race again, but an hour quicker.

Although not scientific, try this unofficial experiment the next time you log on to social media. As you read through your newsfeed, you will see several distinct personalities. You will see the friend posting about yet another one of her car accidents, wondering why drivers are always "so stupid". You see the manager at a reasonably large company complaining he was passed up for another promotion, and if he could only get another job those "idiots in suits" would be shown a thing or two about his ever growing impressive collection of credentials. You see a former coworker creating controversy about political candidates and bashing everything he hates, wondering why nothing goes right in this world anymore.

Then, you have your friend from college who posts the random selfies surrounded by friends or family, with an inspirational quote as a caption. You see them encouraging others via comments and likes, rather than critiquing. They go about their day highlighting positivity and goal setting, showing posts about habits they have (active lifestyle, memories created by deepening relationships, attempting their first homemade apple pie). You look at her profile to see if she is doing well in a field that you somehow "knew" she would always wind up in.

How did that happen? Each person, through the culmination of internal guidance and external stimuli, chose the life they have. Instead of being challenged by limits, they limited their challenges.

> *"At 211°, water is hot. At 212°, it boils. And with boiling water comes steam. And steam can power a locomotive. The one extra degree makes the difference." - Mac Anderson & Sam Parker, authors*

Combining the steam engine quote with Darren Hardy's compound effect, if you change your life one degree and it compounds over years, the difference created becomes leaving a life of legacy versus simply living.

To start, if you consider incremental growth and try to improve your life by 1% a day, then after 100 days you would be 100% improved. But is a 100% improvement realistic? Can you take 24 minutes a day for complete self-improvement? The answer of course, is yes. However, most people have a confliction between what they say and what they actually do. Are you really going to set your alarm 24 minutes early to dedicate time to self-improvement? Are you really able to dedicate 24 extra minutes to playing with your kids before dinner? Are you really able to come up with an extra 2.8 hours a week? Probably not, initially. The good news is there's a butterfly effect to this as well. Also, you don't need to suddenly find that kind of time. The key here is to start incredibly small, make incremental changes, and let momentum build as your building blocks are constructed.

In his book, *Focal Point*, Brian Tracy, explains how to improve any section of your life by 1,000 percent, based on the law of incremental improvement (which the Japanese call the Kaizen principle). His advice is to increase your productivity by simply 1/10 of 1% a day. That's less than three minutes of your day. Anyone can do that! You can be a little more alert during a meeting, you can hug your children a little longer, and you can look your spouse in the eyes and remind them why you love them.

The beauty of Tracy's formula is that it builds tremendous momentum that can extend into all facets of life. Once you start, it is easier and easier to keep going and you naturally get faster and faster. Similarly, if a quarter- sized snowball begins to roll down a steady grade mountain, it grows in size larger and larger.

If you focus a bit more every day 1/10 of 1% for a week (five days), that is 2% improvement. Suddenly, you are actually starting to like the new opportunities that arise. Your life will start to come together more as the new habits you have acquired begin to take shape. After 52 weeks, your life has become 26% more productive and efficient. If you apply 26% a year for 10 years you will be 1,000% better.

Set your goals 1,000% higher than you are now. What does that life look like? What does it feel like? What does it mean to you?

Think of this analogy from Hardy regarding the power of small adjustments. Let's say there is a plane heading to New York City from Los Angeles. If the pilot accidentally or inadvertently adjusts the nose by a mere 1%, the plane will land 150 miles away from NYC in either Dover, Delaware or upstate near Albany. The power of momentum works both ways. In the same way that tiny details can derail your dreams, tiny details can also bring you more than you ever dreamed possible.

But of course, this all starts with your personal decision to try.

> *"Either you deal with what is the reality or you can be sure that the reality is going to deal with you."*- Alex Haley, author

## Making the Decision

> *"What is not started today is never finished tomorrow."* - Johann Wolfgang von Goethe, German Poet

The first step towards anything you want in life begins with making a decision. Then, you can work at making the decision right. Everything in life that currently exists; places, things, people, relationships, food and drink, was at one point just a thought. Everything you see, feel, or touch started as a thought. Then, through a series of events, that thought became reality. Everything in life exists due to a choice that was made at some point.

We will delve into excuses in later chapters, but it is worth noting that most people put off making a key decision due to an excuse they've been carrying around their entire lives. People who don't go after what they want believe that they have a reason to sit back idly. When this happens, the entrepreneurs, athletes, and achievers in our world pass them by. They lose all of their power in their life by not making a decision and not trying. There is nothing embarrassing about falling, like the baby. Nobody critiques a baby for falling after it tries to stand. So why do we critique others for trying to take a stand?

The only thing that should be critiqued is when somebody doesn't attempt to stand. If you have the heart to go out and try for something you believe in, you earn the respect. It takes a bold, strong, person to lead a company or win a medal at the Olympics. Why? Because they are willing to do what others won't. At some point, they make a decision to change their life and they begin to ignite changes that do just that. It doesn't matter if they start with 1% change, they started.

"If you want to know what shifts your business, what shifts your life, there's one force. Decision making." In one of his most popular YouTube clips, Motivational speaker and self-help instructor Tony Robbins says, "Get darnn good at making decisions. Most people don't have the guts to make the tough decisions, because they want to make the right decision, so they make no decision, and that's the decision. And what happens is the world takes them over. So decision making is the power. By the way, leaders make decisions. That's what makes them a leader."

When I was conducting my interviews, I noticed that every successful person was able to relate to one simple philosophy. They all recognized the power of knowing you could create or do something that others didn't believe could be done. When somebody tells you, "that can't be done", they aren't saying that you can't do it. They are saying *they* couldn't. Or somebody they knew couldn't. Something in their life, the decisions they made, the thoughts that went in to their attempt, halted their efforts. They couldn't do it.

Remember, they aren't you. They can't relate to your inner voice. Even if they study your mind, live with you, and socialize with you every weekend, they still can't possibly fathom or predict the choices you will make. They don't know your unique abilities, your talents, and your drive. They don't understand how you are going to pull it off and how you will respond to those quick second decisions that need to be made when adversity comes up. They don't and never will see the same future for you as you see for yourself. THEY AREN'T YOU.

Jeff Shelton, founder and owner of San Diego based Wholesale Warranties, shared his viewpoints on the real failures of life being the lack of ability to make a decision. "I believe that the only people who actually fail are the ones who didn't make a decision to do something in the first place. I'm not talking about abandoning an initiative once you realize it isn't the right thing to do anymore. Rather, if you try to do something and it doesn't work, it's a learning experience and you've learned something new for the next time. I don't really believe there is failure. Just the experience needed to make the next decision better."

Prior to starting Epic Book Launch, Austin Netzley's first business was in an entirely different industry. After taking a year off to travel, he decided to start a blog and podcast. As he was interviewing influential people, he quickly realized there are a lot of commonalities. Many of the interviewees made the same decisions. "I thought that I may be on to something, but nobody knew who I was so I needed a book to be able to reach and inspire people and share my story." That moment was his turning point. He made the decision to write a book.

It took four months to write the book. Then came the hardest part, as any author will share, which was to get his book in the hands of as many people as possible. When Netzley's book, *Make Money Live Wealthy*, became a best-seller, another decision was made. He wanted to help others market their own books. Now, his company is steadily increasing revenue and has hit the million-dollar revenue mark. Furthermore, because of his decision to break free of his past industry and try for something new, Netzley has helped thousands of aspiring authors (including bringing this book to you).

Brad Fowler, CEO of startup Nutraplex, shared "Every single day as an entrepreneur, you have no idea what you're getting into. The problem most people have is a fear of the unknown. This fear causes people to make no decision at all, which will change the direction of their life. Fear isn't even tangible. Fear isn't real. Going into the unknown can be exciting and that's what allowed me to change the world. It's being able to realize that your fear is only going to stop you. It won't stop the other people around you that you are trying to present to or sell to. They don't feel your fear. As soon as someone can conquer that, then they can make decisions and doing things they never thought they could. Most of the time, people have more negative effects from not making any decision than they do making the move and not understanding all the details."

> *"You're never a loser until you quit trying." - Mike Ditka, NFL Head Coach*
>
> *"Anything you really want, you can attain, if you really go after it." - Wayne Dyer, author*
>
> *"When we strive to become better than we are, everything around us becomes better too." -- The Alchemist by Paulo Coelho*
>
> *"If you are not willing to risk the usual you will have to settle for the ordinary."- Jim Rohn, entrepreneur and author*
>
> *"Nothing works unless you do."- Maya Angelou, poet*

**How Practice & Momentum Actually Works**

In his famous novel, *Outliers*, Malcolm Gladwell details his theory that it takes 10,000 hours of deliberate practice to become world-class in any area. Now, when most of us think about practice, we think about doing something repetitively for a length of time just to check it off of our to-do lists. However, that's not the type of practice he's talking about. The word deliberate, changes the very definition of how we should view practice. The concept, advanced by Anders Ericcson and investigated by countless others, has several principles that are key to honing our skills and advancing us in our fields.

In his book, *Talent is Overrated*, Geoff Colvin, breaks down deliberate practice into five key areas. Each one is equally as important as the next. To begin with, deliberate practice is specifically designed to improve performance. When I use to help clients through personal training, people didn't hire me to simply watch them work out. For example, if someone's goal was to lose weight, chances are they already know what to do. They need to eat fewer calories and work out more. Instead, they paid me because a workout with me is practice to fine-tune their lifestyle, allowing them to improve their body and have a higher quality of life. When I trained a client, I intensely focused on their form, tempo, sets, and amount of repetitions that were designed for target areas they needed the most improvement on, in that hour, on that day, in that specific moment of their training calendar. I could see when they were in the eccentric (or lowering phase) of a lift too long, causing unnecessary muscle lengthening. I could tell if they have had long term progress based on manipulating variables of the workout and testing their bodies. And yes, I could tell if they said they wanted to lose weight, but secretly went home and binge ate junk food. I was hired because I could see things my clients couldn't see or wouldn't admit to doing. Things that ultimately shaped their bodies and their futures.

It is no different in your business. You rely on experts to coach and guide you deliberately (and if you don't, you should). "Deliberate practice is created to stretch a particular person out of their current abilities" explains Colvin. Becoming incredibly talented/gifted in any area is extremely difficult if you do not have a coach or an expert guiding you. Experts build their business on providing a clear and unbiased view of their actions.

Think right now about what you are trying to improve on. There may be several (and if you're being honest, there are) key things you need to improve on to enhance your life or your business. Identify one that is absolutely crucial to your future. Now...hire an objective third party to help guide you in that area. Allow them to point out things you may have missed. Allow them to teach you, step by step, what to do. If you meet once a week, turn off your cell phone, devote not just your time but your energy to that lesson. Focus intently. Take in their advice, heed their advice. Practice their advice and let them tell you where your practice needs fine tuning. Don't just show up for the meeting. Anyone can walk into a conference room with an expert and hear somebody speak for an hour. The difference between the world's most successful people and the everyday person is that they listen and adhere to deliberate practice designed to specifically improve performance. They consciously absorb and mentally carry out what they learn.

Another piece of deliberate practice is repetition. When you want to improve an aspect of your life, you can't just make it a one-time event. Look at any idol you have. In *Outliers*, Malcolm Gladwell describes part of the reason for the Beatle's massive success. When they first started playing, long before they were famous, they took several trips to Hamburg where they performed in eight hour intervals. Yes...eight hours. They took their eight hours of performing and made it a full-out practice. The Beatles devoted the entire experience to fine tuning their skills. In order to sustain such a long set, they were forced to evaluate their performances and find a different way to play.

In the early 1960's, the Beatles took five successive trips to Hamburg. In their first trip, they played 106 nights, 7 days a week, for over 5 hours a night. For their second trip, they performed for 92 nights. On the third trip, it is calculated they spent 172 hours on stage. Finally, by the end of 1962 they had an additional 90 hours of performing from their last two trips. If you're adding this up, they performed 270 nights in a year and a half. Naturally, by the time they returned from Hamburg, they were a different band. Every time you focus intently on that practice, you build towards the 10,000 hours' theory. By the time they made it to America in 1964, they had played more than most bands play today. They were talented, but by deliberately practicing over 1,200 times in that window, they were also positioned as leaders in the music scene because they had put in more time than anybody and learned how to fine-tune their abilities to withstand any obstacles that may arise. The deliberate practice made them great.

Another crucial element of deliberate practice is the continuous availability of feedback. This is perhaps the easiest part of practice because feedback is instantaneous. A comedian who delivers a punch line with no laughter instantly knows his joke isn't successful. An athlete can look up at the score and know if they are winning or not. A skilled recruiter calls you after a job interview to tell you what information you shouldn't have shared and what information to share next time. Get and seek out feedback.

Deliberate practice is also highly demanding mentally. Colvin explains, "Deliberate practice is above all an effort of focus and concentration." When you are engaged in deliberate practice, all of your attention and energy is being focused. You aren't just participating to participate. You are there for one reason, to enhance your performance. There are many studies for how long people can sustain such intense focus, but the upper limit is five hours per day.

Anyone can go to a gym and do a few crunches, talk to their friends, use the restroom, do another exercise, ride the bike for 40 minutes and say they were there three hours. But when you deliberately set out to enhance your performance in a gym, you know what exercise to warm up with, how long to do that and at what heart rate, before you even hit the free weight pit. Once there, you know exactly what weight to grab, how to perform the lift with correct form, how many seconds to lift, hold, decrease. You know the amount of repetitions and sets, before moving to the next exercise. You deliberately focus your attention on when to breathe in, when to exhale. You scan the room to identify what machine is next available and position yourself to be there within the 45 second post-lift window. Most people's bodies can't sustain a workout like that for three hours. Top-tier athletes who have been conditioned appropriately through deliberate practice and high focus can.

Lastly, deliberate practice is practice. It isn't much fun. Anytime you do something you are really good at, you tend to smile more and have fun. However, in deliberate practice you mentally focus on improvement. Naturally, if you are good at something, you aren't always trying to improve. It is finding the flaw in our moment and perfecting it. You aren't smiling and giggling. You are focusing. You are performing for enhancement. You are concentrating for improvement. You have a specific goal in mind and you are diverting time, energy, and resources at equal amounts towards that goal for approximately 10,000 hours. You aren't letting adversity kick you down. You can't. You have a finite amount of time to hone in on what you want and you are leveraging practice to get you there.

> *"Perfect practice makes perfect." - Vince Lombardi, NFL head coach*

When I interviewed Steve Mehr, CEO of Webshark 360, he stated, "I think in general most people quit too early and I think that it does take a long time. The way I conduct business now is knowing that I won't make money for 5-10 years, on any new endeavor. Starting out, I was 7 days a week for 7-8 years, putting myself through school at night. What I lacked in knowledge and resources, I made up for in raw hours. All I had was time. That's the mentality a lot of people don't understand. At 21, I had an offer at Microsoft in the mobile computing division paying $150k (which was more than I was making), but I turned it down because I knew I would hit my goals in life. It took me 10 years before I could breathe again and five years before I was finally stable. I've found most people lose sight of that."

He goes on to say, "Building a successful life takes a long time and I haven't found people who are smart enough who can do it within a seven-year window, unless there is a little luck involved. If it's much faster, you can't hold on to it because you can't understand how the whole process works. Fast forward 10 years after their initial success, most of those people are broke."

Gary Vaynerchuk is not just known for being a best-selling author, but also his intense viewpoints on how "no one gets truly wealthy without putting in serious work". Vaynerchuk himself started his entrepreneurial legacy at 13, with a $1,000 loan from his father to resell baseball cards. In an interview with Shopify.com, he shares, "When I was 13 or 14 my father dragged me into the store and I've been pretty much working there until now, when we started VaynerMedia and I'm a little less involved. It was every weekend, every school holiday, and every day of the summer. I was really all-in; I worked every day of my freshman, sophomore, junior and senior year. And I mean every day, literally from the first day of the summer to the last, except for Sundays sporadically."

In an article on Mashable, Nellie Akalp, CEO/Owner/ founder of entrepreneurial consulting company Corpnet Inc. writes, "Start-up founders need persistence be-cause everything always takes longer than expected- often two or three times longer. It can be difficult to keep things going when you're not seeing instant traction and success."

Other proven entrepreneurs agree in the hard work principle. Don Langmo explains it took him roughly 52,000 hours to reach success. Back when he didn't have much money, he only had time. For about 750 weeks of working 70 hours a week, he put in hours. "I developed a habit of working hard all day, every day, and reading everything I could get my hands on. I've never met a successful entrepreneur who didn't read a lot of different things in the time they had away from the office. I can only hear and see so much but there's no limit on what I can read." Entrepreneurs need to know a lot about every facet of their business. They initially need to know about finance, psychology, sales, marketing, organizational design, and the industry. If you made the decision to be proactive about your future and you don't have the resources yet to hire a staff, you have the time. And when you utilize that time efficiently, over many years, one day you will look back at the success you had.

Brad Fowler shares, "When I started Nutraplex, I was like a cat. I was clawing, scraping, and fighting my way out of a battle to just get to the top. It was seven days a week, 12-15 hours a day, wearing multiple hats. We finally started getting traction after about two years (8,736 hours). We had a phenomenal response immediately because it is a great product, but it was really the third year we could cover costs and materials to build our footprint of doctors across the country."

Anthony Mongeluzo, founder and partner of several website developments, SEO, and content marketing companies grew up in southwest Philadelphia. "I got the suit of hard work and entrepreneurship. I had to figure things out. It's not the awards I've won that have led to my success; it's the process and teamwork." The amount of hard work that goes in to creating something from nothing, is grossly underestimated in today's instant-gratification society. "Most people think they can work 16 hours a day, if the opportunity is right. In order to grow something, you need to do anything for years and years to build up. It's not for everyone and it shouldn't be." It took Anthony 5-6 years of 7 days a week. "I literally only took off Thanksgiving and Christmas, but still checked emails on those days. It took quite a while and every time you hit a different level of success, you need to be able to do different things." In the last 18 months, he has brought on an additional 50 employees due to tremendous growth. He knew he had to make a decision to pursue the IT industry and put in years of deliberate practice to make his dreams reality. "I just thought I could do something better and be somebody better, for the IT industry."

A student of Warren Tracey once wrote a famous line that is now taught in most MBA schools. "Entrepreneurship is living a few years of your life like most people won't, so you can live the rest of your life like most people can't." If you continue to work hard, one day all of your hard work will pay off.

> *"If you're not having doubts, you're not pushing the boundaries far enough." - Tony Fadell, CEO of Nest*

Chapter 4

# The Power of YOU

This is the third time in 20 minutes my IV pole beeps suddenly, alerting me that there is air in the line of my port-o-cath. I glance at the clock, 2:32 a.m. You would think that hospitals are a place to rest, recover, and sleep in. During the day there's a host of staff members walking into and out of your room. At night, there's a litany of medications and blood draws to test how the medications are being absorbed in your body. In the past 12 hours, I've had two blood draws, four half-hour respiratory treatments, 38 pills, and a continuous drip of IV antibiotics to destroy the latest bacteria that wants to slowly strip me of my future opportunities. I know I could page the nurse, roll over, and let her deal with my finicky IV pole. Then she'll come in, full of energy after her fifth cup of coffee on graveyard shift, and we will wind up talking about everything that has happened in the two months since I've seen her last.

I opt to try to avoid pulling a hospital all-nighter by fixing it myself. I get up and walk over to my machine. I adjust the settings and flick the air bubbles back up through my central line to the IV drip bag where they belong. I adjust the setting so the alarm isn't mind-numbingly loud and slump back into a pile on my bed.

It's probably weird to admit, but I love nights in the hospital. As my own form of meditation, I slow my breathing in an attempt to get my heart rate as low as possible on the EKG. One night, I accidentally set the alarm off by getting my heart to 35 beats per minute. The nurses and doctors that rushed into my room thinking I was in cardiac arrest didn't find the humor in my game, but I felt victorious.

Despite the blue lights glowing from my various machines, my room is dark. Even the hallways are dimly lit in an attempt to help other patients sleep. The sound of my lungs working for once penetrates the emptiness. In every room, there is an eerie silence with the exception of a random Code Blue emergency that, in a twisted way, reminds me to be thankful that my cheeks still have color in them.

I open my eyes, glance around the room, relishing in my thankfulness to still have such vitality after 28 years of being told next year might not happen. I have my blanket from home, my lucky teddy bear, a stack of personal development books, and my own pillow. On the shelf next to my pill cup are two dozen roses my boyfriend brought me yesterday. This hospitalization is relatively easy, but every night I can't help but wonder if the roses will outlive me.

It's important to allow myself time to realize how precious our lives are. It's important I spend the nights I can't sleep here thinking about how much I love my life outside of these walls. When you are grateful for every moment, no matter how good or bad, you just want another moment. You quit capitalizing on only the good stuff because the bad stuff is still a reminder that there is air in your lungs, power in your existence.

I need a walk. Without even needing to turn on the light, I unhook myself from the drip. I know where to find the cap to my line and how to disconnect myself from my machines. It's unusually warm in my room, but I still put on a sweater. Not only does it conceal the needle sticking out of my chest, but dressing like a visitor instead of a patient is an affirmation to me that tonight I won't be one of those code blues.

I peak outside the door to make sure the nurses aren't at their stations. They've really become more than hospital staff, they are friends. They are confidants. They have been there for me when visitors weren't able to make it. They even were there for me several years ago when a guy I was dating dumped me via text because, "dating somebody with Cystic Fibrosis is too hard". They are there for me on birthdays, Thanksgivings, Christmases, and New Year's Eves. Sometimes though, just sometimes, I need the quiet the hospital brings.

My mind continues racing back and forth between past and future as I saunter down the hall, away from their station, into the back stairway that the night security guard showed me months ago. The nostalgia of what has happened since my last stay here makes me feel empty. Trying to set goals for my future makes me feel anxious.

I set my phone alarm to go off at 3:30a.m. so I'm back by my next round of IV's. My mind continues to drift. I think intensely and widely, without abandon. I'm genuinely happy here. I wonder if that's what happens when criminals get locked up for periods of time, they become institutionalized. I can't imagine a life without these walls every few months. I take what I can get when I'm out, but when I'm here and my body is getting healthier, there's tranquility. The friendships I've created, some of the best memories of my life, have been here. I can't think this same way when I am at home, too many distractions. The most inspirational moments of my life have occurred within the emptiness of a hospital hallway at 3 a.m.

I know that statistically I am much older than I should be. I also know that statistically more people die in hospitals than in their own homes. Statistically, these deaths occur between 11p.m. and 4 a.m. There is a power to being able to walk the halls at that exact time and place, knowing that it has the highest chance that I will go home through the morgue instead of through the main entrance. I start to really let that sink in. There is power right now, in every breath. That breath is a signal to my mind that I'm not the statistic.

I firmly believe, against all odds, that it's not my time. I've had some close calls. I'll probably have more of them. But there's so much more to my life, my legacy, my story. I have so much to experience and so many things I want to do for the world. I'll leave this hospital a stronger version of myself. Soon I will be able to start creating my future, leveraging the power of others who think like I think, and maybe one day, create something worthy to share with this world.

Right in the middle of my inner monologue, doctors and nurses rush past me through the halls in a frenzied run. The lights in the hallway auto adjust and the speakers boom through the silence "Code Blue, Code Blue. Attention staff on 2 West, there is a Code Blue in room 211".

I close my eyes and offer up a prayer of gratitude that I am still alive. I just hope whoever was in room 211 was able to truly appreciate the moments they had in life. I hope they had a chance to tell their loved ones' goodbye. I hope they realized that life isn't measured by the number of breaths we take, but by the number of moments that take our breath away.

## The Power of the Subconscious Mind

*"Whether you think you can, or think you can't--you're right." - Henry Ford, Founder Ford Motor Company*

It seems like everyone these days knows about the power that can manifest from cultivating your thoughts towards what you want the world to be like. It's a story we've all heard time and time again. If you're broke, struggling, newly single, lost your job...the list goes on and on...just close your eyes and think deeply about what you want your life to be like. Think about what you want your life to feel like. Imagine a situation where you walk into your dream job. What do the floors look like as you walk? How does it sound as your dress shoes rhythmically hit the tiles? What does the assistant say as she greets you? How do you reply? What does the feeling in the pit of your stomach feel like? Simple exercises like this promise to bring you the exact moment you've dreamed of. However, if you're a skeptic like I once was, you're going to need a bit more information about the law of attraction before you rush out to the craft store to start putting together your visualization board.

To start, grab something to write with. I'm not joking. I thought this was fluff when I heard it for the first time too, but it works. Read through the following three steps and complete the exercise below:

*Step 1: Without scanning the room, shut your eyes and recall everything you could see that is red.*

*Step 2: Write it down. Do NOT look around the room.*

*Step 3: When you are finished, tally up how many items you wrote down.*

Now, open your eyes and spend 30 seconds looking around the room for everything you see that is red. The pen you're holding? A candle? Fire hydrant? Apple? Someone's shirt? Red is suddenly "everywhere" around you. After these 30 seconds are over, without looking back up, write down all the things you now see. Notice how now that you know what to look for, red seems to be everywhere. That's how our mind works. When we know what we are looking for, when we consciously focus our attention and energy into searching for it, we see it. We see things that have been right in front of our noses all along. We just didn't know they were there.

Your mind is more powerful than it even has the ability to understand. Everything you see in this room once started as a thought from somebody else. Each item was a mere dream. When your inner voice matches your subconscious, you will be amazed at how things seem to come together.

Louis Spagnuolo, brand ambassador for Rolls Royce and Chairman of the Board for Illuminati Trust, strongly believes in the power of selecting your thoughts. When he is asked about tips for success, Spagnuolo is quick to reference the law of attraction. "Many people don't apply the mental principle to their success."

The mind is a muscle in the same way as the biceps are. If you are at the gym, conditioning your body through lifting, you experience hypertrophy. Growing your mind works in a similar way. "The brain manifests what your future becomes. Whether it's the law of attraction or envisioning what you want, use the universe to help bring it to you," Spagnuolo shares. Use free weights to build your biceps, use free thinking to build your brain.

Of course, that's much easier to say than to actually do. Where does one start? Spagnuolo shares how he manifests his reality by conditioning his mind to attract what he wants in life. "Let the universe dictate the direction you're going but condition your mind to bring things into your life." You must have a clear vision. Identify and write down what goals and ambitions you have. Without a vision, you're like a ship in the middle of the ocean without an engine. You are aimlessly floating in the current. There are many times he found himself trying to manifest something and when it didn't happen he was disappointed. He would think about how hard he worked for something, frustrated that it never happened. However, something else would come along and afterwards the result would be so much greater than he ever anticipated. Sometimes the universe just needs to take the control. Your mind steers the direction of wanting to sail, but the universe dictates what island you land on.

Spagnuolo also doesn't believe in putting time limits on things, preferring to leave that to the universe. "Time limits do more than limit time, they limit yourself and success." When you trust things will work out in appropriate time, you can spend your resources on other techniques such as physical wellbeing and attitude.

He isn't alone either. Interestingly enough, out of the 50 interviews completed for this book, just about every single person from a variety of nationalities, backgrounds, religious affiliations, gender, and sexual orientation all mentioned the law of attraction at some point.

In the first two minutes of his interview, author of *Conscious Millionaire*, JV Crum III, shared that he decided he was a millionaire when he was just five years old. "One thing I noticed is when I got clear as a boy, that I would be a millionaire, I believed it 100%. I didn't entertain any other thought other than this is where I'm headed and this is the world I want.'"

Crum wasn't born with a silver spoon in his mouth, far from that. His dream came when his mother told him he couldn't have a piece of candy at the grocery store because it was too expensive. When Crum turned eight, he had this feeling like he was in the wrong place, with the wrong family. "I was constantly reimagining who I was, what I was capable of, and where I was headed, without any concern or thought on how I would get there. I believed completely I was right and what I was seeing, I was creating."

In his 20's, he still clung to his vision of being a millionaire. This drive got him through a time in his life when he was a starving graduate student with a budget of $5 a week for food. "I never in any way doubted I would get there. I constantly was reprogramming my mind, and on a daily basis I was envisioning my future, which had nothing to do with the world I was living in."

Even as we were talking, he had behind him a whiteboard with his vision on it. Many times, he would look up, trusting the perfect timing of the universe. Energy is around all of us, all of the time. That's simple physics. The world is filled with connectivity and energy and all of that information is available. In all aspects of life, it is what the mind chooses to believe that shapes the destiny your life takes.

### Understanding the Four Learning Stages

When I was a teenager my mom took me to an empty parking lot and handed me the keys to drive for the very first time. I was nervous. I grew up driving ATV's across Iowa farmland, but a manual transmission pickup truck was intimidating. I didn't know what I needed to know. The first time I let my foot off the clutch the car bucked forward so fast that I felt like I would fly straight through the windshield, had my seatbelt not stopped me. I didn't even know what I didn't know. I was afraid, embarrassed to make mistakes, and had absolutely no self-confidence. I knew so little, that I basically knew nothing.

According to many psychologists, there are four stages to learning that apply across all aspects of life. Many entrepreneurs start out their adventure in the first stage, unconsciously incompetent. They are just like I was when I was learning how to drive. They have no idea what to do once handed the keys to a business. This is also the phase people start out in when they head to the gym as their New Year's resolution. They aren't familiar with the equipment. They aren't aware of what they should be eating. They are completely lost. This is when your "why" mentioned earlier becomes important. In this stage, it has been estimated that roughly 8 out of 10 people give up. However, when the "why" behind driving a car, starting a company, or entering the gym reminds your subconscious to press on, then you make it to the second stage, consciously incompetent.

In this stage, you do repetitive work. You practice long and you practice often. You may even find yourself implementing deliberate practice (as mentioned earlier as well). If you want to drive a car, first you circle a parking lot and practice parking the vehicle. If you're starting a company, you start to learn about all of the back office work that you weren't aware needed to be discovered. If you're in a gym, you read the instructions on the machines and begin to push yourself. It is in this phase; you think to yourself, "Geez, I know nothing." Now you know what you don't know and you know somewhat what you need to know. As you repeat what you steadily learn, you move into phase three, also known as consciously competent.

This is the phase where you are suddenly aware of what you are doing. You become good at something, but you can't do it with your eyes closed. You can signal a turn, but if a squirrel jumps across the road, you still have to mentally decide if you should hit it or slam on the brakes. You can join an entrepreneur's organization, but before you volunteer to chip in to the conversation, you really need to actively focus on the questions and what the other group members need in an answer. At the gym, you certainly can use the machine now, but if somebody comes up to you to say "hello" you get out of your rhythm. This stage requires active focus. This stage requires purposeful action and mental preparation. This is the stage associated most with effort, every action and reaction requires thought.

"Lack of success, draws most people out in this stage," shares Larry Linne. Linne is also a certified soccer coach in addition to CEO of InCite Performance Group. "Kids come out to practice and think they can kick a ball easily. You teach them how to properly have their foot hit the ball and kids will fail trying to kick it with correct form. Many quit, but what we do is slowly work repetition in. The way we get them through it, is by adding pressure. We make them dribble first, and then kick it. Now we add somebody chasing them. Now we put another player in front of them. We continue to change variables and add pressure and it teaches them to cognitively deal with the circumstances."

Sometimes, people get so good at this learning stage that they become complacent and get passed up by competition without even realizing it, causing them to slide back down. It makes no difference whether you are a kid learning to kick a soccer ball or an adult starting a company. You must be prepared to move through the learning stages and accept the feedback you see along the way. You need to be aware of what you don't know, and open to learning about it.

If somebody hasn't given up by now, usually this stage can be the defining moment or breaking point. However, if the reason behind an action is strong enough, they can move into the fourth stage, known as being unconsciously competent. In this phase, you are really great at something without needing to think about it. This is the stage where people enjoy driving because it gives them time to relax and think. This is the zone athletes get in when they are in a state of bliss and their mind can wander while they are practicing. This is the CEO who can now mentor others, because when a situation arises, they instinctively know how to correct it. The only way to get here is through focus and deliberate practice. The unconscious is infinitely more powerful when you build it through forced repetition.

Think for a moment, what color are yield signs? If you said yellow, you are wrong. When I tried this exercise for the first time, I was wrong too. When I started driving, they were yellow. However, it has been over 10 years since they changed to red. Our subconscious is that powerful. Something that happened a decade ago, that we see every day, we can't remember.

When your mind knows what to look for, everything you do changes. For example, meetings with clients become a lot easier when you walk in knowing what the purpose of the meeting is, what the client needs from you, and how you can satiate that need. You begin to live a life that is goal-oriented and purposeful, as opposed to random encounters where you scramble to put together information. Now, the information is put together for you and you see the pieces of the puzzle as clues to the picture you are trying to create.

> *"Your inner dialogue will either fuel your success or prevent you from reaching your true potential."- Anonymous*
>
> *"What the mind can conceive, the mind can achieve and those who stay will be champions." - Bo Schembechler, American football player and head coach*

### Power of High Self Esteem

Have you ever thought about the little messages you are sending your subconscious throughout the day? Let's say, you have a goal to be healthier this year and you decide to accomplish this goal by not eating out and going to the gym three times a week.

What do you do when you cheat on your goal by eating out and skipping the gym? What do you tell yourself? If you're like most people, you have extreme guilt and take your mind down a negative path. You already know you messed up, but you repeat that mistake over and over in your head. When you weigh yourself the next Monday without seeing any results, you tell yourself that your lack of willpower is why you are fat. You tell yourself that it doesn't matter what goals you set, you can't achieve them. You reinforce that you have no willpower and you're going to stay unhealthy because you just can't get over how great pizza tastes. You're upset that you can't seem to find the time to squeeze in workouts and that you must not know how to prioritize your life.

Sounds pretty accurate, right? But here's the thing. What would you tell your best friend if they called you and mentioned they skipped the gym and ate out? Probably that it's okay to have a slip up as long as they can correct it and learn from it. You will probably tell him or her that it's understandable because you know how stressful their job is and they just needed to have a sausage mushroom pie on their lunch break for sanity. You encourage them to pick right back up because you know they can accomplish their goal. Just because they had a bad meal doesn't mean they're a bad person.

Do you talk to yourself the way you talk to your friends? Are you sending yourself self-defeating messages on a regular basis and then blaming yourself when those self-defeating messages come true? As you start the momentum of negative self- talk, you cultivate more negativity, which results in decreased performance, which then circles back to even more negative self-talk. This is a downward spiral. Most of the time you don't even realize you are doing this. The good news is that you can build yourself up the same way you tear yourself down.

Self-esteem has a lot to do with how honest you are about yourself. Only you know your true abilities, talents, and how hard you work to make your goals your reality. Only you know how much love and respect you put into your personal relationships. Only you know how much time out of the office you dedicate to fitness and hobbies. Only you know if you are truly maximizing your time in the office. If you are wasting your time painting a picture of somebody who doesn't really exist when you look in the mirror, your self-esteem will suffer.

> *"I am not what happened to me. I am what I choose to become."* Emma Watson, actress
>
> *"If you think of defeat, you are bound to be defeated."* - *Anonymous*

There is a lot of interpretation for how the power of positive thinking and self-esteem works. And it works differently for everyone. A few months ago, I was leaving a speaking engagement when an audience member asked me, "if being positive really worked, why do you still have Cystic Fibrosis?"

I am not at all saying that the power of positive thinking can cure ailments, especially genetic diseases. What I am saying is that my outlook on life, my positive attitude, and shaping my thoughts around my daily medical hurdles, has played an essential role in my ability to form a successful recruiting company, being incredibly fit, and authoring a book on entrepreneurship at an age that is beyond the median life expectancy for somebody diagnosed with my disease. I thrive off of feeling like a winner by reminding myself that I am and can be whatever I choose. If I am feeling down, I personally am less motivated to go to the gym. When I skip the gym, I feel less likely to do my treatments, because I rationalize that I'm already doing harm so one treatment doesn't matter. It is my philosophy that lazy days, on rare occasions, can be good. What isn't okay are lazy weeks. Lazy weeks break the power of habit (detailed later) and the downward spiral begins. I have to push myself every day and mentally remind myself of what I am capable of. My mind is stronger than I will ever know. And so is yours.

When I have a positive attitude, when I am fighting to retain my lung function, it is because I believe I deserve a long life and I make better choices. I have full intentions of enjoying my deepest breaths, because even though we can all check out of the office and take a vacation, Cystic Fibrosis doesn't. The day I take a vacation is the day I decided to not be in relentless pursuit of my own longevity. Every day I must find a way to get into a positive state of mind. I can't control the disease, but I can control my mood. My lung function has a direct correlation to my self-esteem. When I feel good, when I am happy, when life is going well, I go longer between hospitalizations. I can't explain it, but it works. And I chose to be happy for the time I get outside of the hospital walls rather than reflect on how horrible it is to spend four months to six months a year inside them.

You can absolutely shape your circumstances by believing in yourself. You have to be your own biggest fan, because if you aren't, then you are leaving your life in the hands of other people. Other people can't design your best life, because they are busy designing their own lives.

There are several techniques for how you can improve your self-esteem. Boomer Esiason relies on being the best prepared person in any situation to build his confidence. "For me, as a football player, my greatest strength was being prepared in the field of play. Before every game, I knew my playbook and opponents. I knew their game plan. And I knew it better than they did; even my own teammates knew that. I adopted an all in mentality, in whatever I did. It's easy to fall back on preparation and be ready for whatever is going to be thrown at you."

To prepare for games, every night Esiason watched game videos, read statistics, and researched elements of the upcoming games. "Let's say we were playing the Steelers; I want to look for all of their tendencies. In football, teams that have success tend to perform similar plays over and over again. You must spend the extra time required to be successful on the field by knowing those tendencies. The more prepared you are, the more poised you are in a high anxiety situation. Great athletes see through anxious moments, allowing their abilities to be played through." When you are in a high pressure situation, the mind can only respond to the pressure. If you aren't fully prepared, the body can't do what it is capable of doing because it is so concentrated on being overwhelmed and anxious. "A characteristic of a great quarterback is poise.You have to be prepared, and that will give you the poise and calmness you need to perform your best in those situations."

"Some days you're not throwing the ball right. There is a human element in sports and how you react in a bad day is ultimately how you will be defined. My advantage came from always being prepared and knowing what the situation was. Even if we lost, it was by a smaller amount than other teams because their quarterbacks weren't as prepared as I was." Esiason had a 14-year career in the NFL as a quarterback for the Cincinnati Bengals, New York Jets, and Arizona Cardinals. During that time, he was a four-time Pro Bowl quarterback, was awarded NFL's Most Valuable Player in 1988, and was one of the most successful quarterbacks in NFL history.

Upon retiring from the NFL, he commentated Monday Night Football for two years. He joined CBS Sports in 2002 as a studio analyst for "The NFL Today" and in 2007 hosted WFAN's national weekday morning radio show, "Boomer and Carton in the Morning."

You must develop a solid work ethic to believe you deserve success. Once you believe you deserve it, your self-esteem is less likely to ride up and down with the inevitable ebbs and flows.

A classic study by Lenore Jacobson, an elementary school principal in San Francisco, and Robert Rosenthal, a Harvard psychologist, tested this very concept. In 18 different classes, ranging from second to fifth grade, Harvard cognitive tests were handed out and completed by the children. Then Rosenthal chose 20% of the students at random and identified them as having "unusual intellectual gains." Rosenthal and Jacobson shared the results with the teachers, identifying which students may appear normal now, but had scored unusually intelligent.

Their actions led to a self-fulfilling prophecy for these students, because their teachers suddenly believed they were gifted. The teachers demanded more, engaged with them more, and enhanced their learning development. The teachers were often "warmer" to these students, giving them more challenging assignments, calling on them more frequently in class, and giving them constructive feedback throughout the year.

So how did their scores actually change? The random 20% of students that showed no actual intellectual genius on the Harvard cognitive test, in the course of one year, improved by an average of 12 IQ points. They outperformed the other students by approximately 15 IQ points in the first grade and 10 IQ points in the second grade. When retested two years later, they were still outperforming their peers.

The only difference between these *"gifted"* students and the other children were the perception that they had more potential by their teacher. Teacher expectations relating to student self-esteem have been studied in several cases and each case had similar results. When a teacher thinks a student is gifted, they become just that.

In *Give and Take* by Adam Grant (Penguin Books, 2013), Grant shows several case studies of what happens to ordinary people when they believe they have high potential. For example, he shares the story of C.J. Skender, a middle-aged accounting professor with trademarked bow ties and a poster of 50 Cent in his office. Skender has earned more than two dozen major teaching awards, taught over 600 classes, evaluated over 35,000 students. His classes are so popular, even his 8 a.m. course once had 190 people on the wait-list. Duke University and The University of North Carolina agreed to give up their rivalry for him, allowing him to teach on both campuses.

Many psychologists have believed that success depends on talent first and motivation second. Skender however, believes everyone has potential so he provides students with mentoring, support, and resources to grow and achieve that potential. Skender looks for motivation and work ethic, rather than simply talent.

It is the approach that every student, as Grant explains, is a "diamond in the rough" that has produced extraordinary results for those who take Skender's course. In the late 1990's to early 2000's, both the silver and bronze medalists on the CPA exam in North Carolina were students of his. In fact, out of 3,396 candidates who took his exam, the top three scores were students he taught. In addition, although a male-dominated field, the top three were women. In his career so far, Skender has had over 40 students win CPA medals by placing in the top three in several different states.

Professors like Skender and teachers like the ones in Rosenthal and Jacobson's study implemented, in one way or another, and maintained positive reinforcement for students. They created significance for the group, making them feel like they were part of something important. The students genuinely believed they had talent and potential. They learned, perhaps on an unconscious level, that self-esteem has to be earned to be valuable, so they put in the extra effort and time. They worked tirelessly. They made sacrifices with their end goal in mind. They were guided by people they looked up to. When your idol tells you that you can achieve something you desperately want, you put in the extra effort. Each successful student saw their significance from the eyes of somebody who mattered to them, and that made the difference.

*"A diamond is just coal under pressure"- Anonymous*

Of course it takes more than just believing in yourself to achieve greatness. You actually have to put in the work behind it. You have to believe you can win more than you believe you can fail. By the same token, you have to have a plan and "grit" that you work towards. This grit is what propels you forward and solidifies your belief in yourself during those moments when things aren't going as planned. When that happens, you can persevere because you have enough to fall back on mentally. A setback is a comeback. And you're in control of all of this.

Life doesn't always go the way you want or expect it to. However, you have the same 24 hours in a day as everyone else. Time is our most finite resource. Entrepreneurs and elite athletes make that time count by focusing on their visions and the positive things. They do not dwell on the negative, they do not complain. They view life as a puzzle where they can put pieces together and move on.

Successful people objectively look at obstacles as if they were a third party, removing the emotion behind it. They set limits and distance themselves. They distance themselves from negative people. They distance themselves from anything they can't fix or find a solution to fix. They don't complain about being overweight while eating another donut. Rather, they identify why they are binge eating and focus to change their situation.

As they take control of every situation and every response they have to stimuli, they slowly gain self-esteem. Here's a tip...NOBODY...and I mean nobody...has it all together. We all struggle, we all look at other people and wish we could be more like them in one way or another. We all want more and to see if more is possible. We all want to believe in our dreams becoming reality, because it signifies our greatest potential as a human. It signifies we are unique and gives us a blueprint for how to live our lives.

When you study today's most influential entrepreneurs and athletes, you'll discover that many consciously focus on building their self-esteem by getting rid of any thought that doesn't serve them. Only then are they able to start focusing on what they can fix and leverage what they have to get where they want to go.

For example, Rick Pitino and Bill Reynolds discuss the power of self-esteem in their book, *Success is a Choice*. "We all want to have more control over our lives. We all want to feel as though we're on the path to becoming more successful, complete with a road map to get us there. We all need a plan of attack and it starts with self-esteem." They observe, "You can expect great things from people who feel good about themselves. They can push themselves. They can set long-term goals. They have dreams that everyone expects to be fulfilled. People with high self-esteem are risk takers, but more important, they are achievers."

Just the opposite is true as well. If people have low self-esteem, they tend to be undisciplined or disorganized and they tend to underachieve. It's tough to associate with people who have low self-esteem because, just like the compound effect to achieve greatness, it creates a negative life. Misery loves company and the cycle continues until they wake up one day, depressed about where they wound up.

Whatever you say about yourself becomes reality. Next time you catch yourself filling your head with negative clutter about yourself, step away as a third party. If you were a friend, would you talk to you the way you currently are? Would you be your own friend?

Let's say for a moment that you are trying to lose weight. Telling yourself you are fat isn't going to help. The next time you are faced with a decision to make regarding a cheeseburger or salad, you can hear your mental voice saying, "Well, you're fat already. One salad won't make a difference. Go for the burger." Here's the thing...that one salad makes all the difference. When you eat better, you feel better. You feel better about yourself. You are more inclined to make healthy decisions again.

You may even feel the need to go up and down the stairs as opposed to always taking the elevator. Sure, you're overweight today. You don't need to be overweight your entire life. With a plan, positive self-belief, and actions, your weight will change.

## The Power of Trusting Yourself

Andre' Phillipe van den Broeck, founder of Dallas clothier offering high-end men's custom suits, shares, "I can't tell you the chain of events that happened (regarding my success). It started quickly and stopped quicker. I lost everything. My cars were repossessed, my place had no electricity. I didn't know how I would feed my dog, let alone myself. That was my moment, sitting on the floor and in tears, holding my dog. I didn't call my parents for help, I didn't call anybody. I just knew that I had to be something. Success is a choice. I realized very quickly sitting there crying, regretful on decisions and wondering what could have been, wouldn't fix the issue. It was a defining moment where I learned I had to get up, roll up the sleeves, and figure it out." Andre' had an inner compass of confidence that led him to taking a stand for his future, and we all have it. We just need to listen to it.

What we listen to dictates our thoughts. In countless interviews, many of the entrepreneurs and athletes shared with me that they don't care what other people think about their dreams and visions. "If we have an idea and you're too small minded to think it's real, that's on you and it has nothing to do with us. We have a heightened level of passion about life and everything that goes on it. We truly think anything is possible. Anything in the world. "Anything." Andre' goes on to say. "I'm a big believer that everything starts in your head. The first battle you must win is between your ears. The bigger your dreams get, the more people tell you that you can't do something, and the more it will require of you to make it happen." To make it today, you have to wake up every day and believe you are built for this and you will get what you want.

Don Langmo, founder of Healthcare Support shares, "Success requires you to believe in yourself. If you have that, and you keep working hard, you'll find a way. I'm a big history buff and grew up reading stories and biographies. In my mind, business is the only exciting adventure that's left. You can't discover new cities or build new things. Business is the last frontier where you can create something from nothing. There are no boundaries and you can create your own new world. It isn't settled yet and you can build something new and different." He trusts in his ability to create new frontiers and when faced with challenges, it is his internal self-confidence that helps him make decisions that shape his future.

Blake Cavignac, founder of YoungPro Elite, shared "Never let other people's perceptions of failures or rejections keep you down. It comes down to conditioning your mind. I think the most successful people have a different view of failure versus success. Success is doing the right things and knowing that nothing will stop them from achievement. Success may not happen as originally planned, but achievers keep going, keep tweaking, and figure it out. Eventually, whether or not you will be successful isn't even up for the conversation. It becomes inevitable." Everything comes back to conditioning. Most people do not dedicate enough time to that psychology.

These entrepreneurs are right. Nobody can believe in the power of your dream more than you do. When adversity roars its head, you must rely on yourself. You must have an internal compass guiding what you can achieve and utilize that to steer you through tough waters. We live in a time where the world changes overnight. We have discovered most, if not all, of the land Earth has. Entrepreneurs are discoverers and creators. If they don't believe in themselves, what they want to discover or create for future generations, then when trouble arises, the foundation will not be in place to persevere.

Martin Grunburg, author of the best-selling book 'The Habit Factor' believes in the quote "The best way to predict the future is to create it." The responsibility falls on the individual. Everybody is dealt a particular hand, but how it's played is up to us.

> *"The mind is its own place, and in itself can make a heaven of hell, a hell of heaven."* - Paradise Lost *by John Milton*
>
> *"If you can imagine it, you can achieve it; if you can dream it, you can become it." - William Arthur Ward, American poet*

Chapter 5

# The Power of Affirmations

Successful entrepreneurs and athletes have affirmations they repeat to themselves. Entrepreneur and author, John Assaraf once stated, "Our jobs as humans is to hold on to the thoughts of what we want, make it absolutely clear in our minds what we want, and from that we start to invoke one of the greatest laws in the Universe, and that's the law of attraction. You become what you think about most, but you also attract what you think about most."

So how do you build your own mantra? How do you come up with a saying that attracts what you think about most? If you can have a thought in your head, you can hold that reality in your hands.

The good news is there are several ways to transform what is in your head into a tangible form. If you are new to this, a good place to start is to create a written out list of daily affirmations. For example, the day I decided that I wanted to be a public speaker and author, I put a pink post-it note by my computer that said, "I am a highly sought after and well-respected public speaker and author." I had absolutely no idea how I would make that happen. I just knew one day, it had to absolutely happen. It was the same thing with my recruiting company. I've had a vision board that read "I own a highly successful recruiting company that helps other high-growth companies."

Create a list on paper. Do not type it. Do not think about doing it. Physically put your hand around a pen and write out what visions you have for your future. As you accomplish them, rewrite the list. Get yourself into the habit of rewriting this list daily. You may go months without ever crossing something off, you may go years. However, every morning when you sit at your desk with your coffee, spend five minutes rewriting a list that will dictate from your conscious to your subconscious what to look for and expect.

In his book, *Conscious Millionaire*, JV Crum III gives some great advice.

> *"Energy and passion fills you with new possibilities for your life and business. You feel powerful and become more committed to achieving at your highest level.*
>
> *People who achieve millionaire wealth and fulfillment let go of anything that has held them back in their past. They choose to become aware of any internal roadblocks, make a conscious decision to move past them, and then focus on taking the actions that will create the results they want.*
>
> *They claim their power, move through any fear, and hold themselves accountable for what they accomplish in their business and life. As a result, they experience significantly higher levels of wealth and success." - JV Crum III*

## Your Ship and Your Crew

Think of the mind as a ship in the ocean. It rolls with the currents, floats in the direction of the wind, and is beaten down by severe storms. In clear weather, it bobs up and down without any real movement. A ship left completely unattended will eventually sink. The ship may float for a while, but guess what it will never do? Reach its destination. It needs more than external forces to get to where it needs to go.

Think of your subconscious as your ship's crew. Your crew knows what harbor to steer towards and what steps to take in order to make sure you reach the destination. When weather is intense, the crew navigates the stormy waters and keeps the ship on course. At all times, regardless of current, wind, and weather, the crew knows where you are and the destination to reach. You need a crew that is confident in navigating all conditions, confident in their abilities, and ready for the unknown. If the ship veers off course, they realign it with the final destination.

As you embark on your dreams, you need a solid crew. You need your subconscious to be on high alert for anything that can get you closer to your destination. If you don't have a crew in place, you will sink. You will not reach your dreams. Without your crew, you are a ship lost at sea.

After time, you will find that writing your affirmations and repeating them daily produce insight that you realize was there all along but you still couldn't manage to find it. In much the same way as you close your eyes and can't see red without knowing what to look for, your affirmations will help you see the red all around you.

As you may expect, just writing out your affirmations isn't enough. You need to see and feel them as well. You need to intensely visualize what your future holds. One way to do this is by creating a vision board. Grab magazines, Google images, get on Pinterest...find the life you want in several categories and glue that life on a poster board. Frame that life. Put that life where you can see it every day and train your mind to get ready for it.

To help you get started, I will share with you my vision board, which sits just to the right of my computer. I have it broken up into four categories: my business (Landmark Makers), my public speaking dreams, my relationships, and my health. My business section is full of quotes from Entrepreneur Magazine and SUCCESS Magazine. There is a handmade organizational chart, which I can't wait to fill up as I hire on more employees due to continued demand for talent acquisition strategies and implementation. My speaking section has a blonde, eyes full of passion, and speaking to a large crowd. On the table to her right, it appears there are several books, which she will in my mind, be signing for her fans. Next to it I wrote, "I am a best-selling author and sought after speaker." My relationship section is full of family photos, best friends, and my dream engagement ring. I wrote in, "I am living with my best friend in America's finest city. I am happily engaged to my partner in a loving and giving relationship. I am enjoying time with my family". Lastly, my health section is my last scores that determine my lung function with the quote "I am healthy". Notice how everything starts with I am?

It's one thing to write your affirmations on paper and carry it with you. It's another level to stare at the visions on a poster board. Elevating your life one more step, close your eyes and imagine what all of that feels like as it is happening.

Every day I spend time imagining how it feels to be speaking at some of the events I have on my list. I imagine the title "Best Selling Author" appearing on the projector as I step on stage. I feel how slick the stage is under my heels, and for a brief moment I am glad I practiced walking in heels before the event. I can see the faces of the people who I have helped in the crowd. I get a burst of butterflies in my stomach because of the energy in the room. I can hear the applause. I imagine the excitement of people coming up and saying how much of an impact I've had on their lives and businesses.

When you try this, get detailed. Whether you are trying to scale your business or scale Everest, imagine the way things sound, the way things feel, the people you will meet, the people you want to meet. Imagine what success looks and feels like. Imagine how you feel during it— the nerves, the happiness, the gratitude.

If you're struggling with this step, as many do when they first start, imagine you were called on next week to write a speech following an award you received in your field. What would you say as you accept? Who would you thank for your success? What type of crowd is peering at you? What are you going to wear? Where is the event? These are great starting tips to help you get a feel for your imagination.

You must have clearly defined goals and you must pursue them every day with enthusiasm. You must believe in yourself more than you believe in anyone else. You must be prepared to explore and create to your heart's content. You must be prepared to have the right people enter your life, exit your life, and shape your life. Failure at some point is inevitable. You must have self-confidence to get through adversity. Realize people are not going to reject you personally, and take that criticism constructively.

Influential people are deliberate goal-setters. In "Rich Habits" by Thomas Corley, he states that 62% of wealthy people focus on their goals every day, as opposed to 6% of poor people—and 67% of the wealthy put those goals in writing.

When you create goals, come up with an audacious long term vision. Then methodically break it down into several manageable, sizable chunks of smaller goals. This is the way, according to Corley, the majority of wealthy people create daily to-do lists—81% of them, in fact, compared to 19% of poor people. Corley also discovered that 67% of wealthy folks actually complete 70% or more of their to-do lists every day.

In a study conducted in 2007, researchers discovered how effective writing down goals was. One hundred forty nine people aged between 23 and 72 years old, from many different backgrounds and cultures, were divided up into five groups.

Group one was asked to *think* about goals they'd like to accomplish over the next four weeks and reflect on the importance of the goal. Group two, instead, was told to *write down* their goals and reflect on why they were important. Group three was instructed to write down their goals as well as actions they could take to achieve them. Group four was instructed to write down their goals, reflect on them, create actionable steps, and communicate the actionable items with a supportive peer. Group five was instructed to do everything from the other groups, but to include weekly progress reports to the supportive peer. Perhaps it will come as no surprise Group five accomplished 78% more of their goals than group one did.

Each successful person has their own methodology to setting their goals. What's important is finding a strategy that works for you and sticking to it. Joel Brown, founder of Addicted2Success.com, calls for a prioritized "To-Do List" every evening before going to bed to prepare for the next day. Twitter co-founder Jack Dorsey believes Sunday is an important day for organization and a time to "get ready for the rest of the week."

We all know the power of goals, but what we sometimes forget, is the power of working backwards from a dream to a goal. First by focusing on behaviors within us, we can identify what we want to change.

To help you get started, I will explain how I utilized this backwards approach when I first started as a recruiter to determine what I needed to do every day, consistently, to reach the income I wanted to generate. At the time, I was making $13 an hour, but my realistic first year earnings dream was $100,000 a year. Knowing long term success is simply a compilation of small decisions we make every day, I divided that $100,000 into how many sales I could make every month. The average commission was $2,500 per person that signed a job offer.

$100,000 / $2,500 = 40 placements needed.

40 placements needed / 12 months = 3.3 a month to hit my goal. For math purposes and because I like a challenge, let's say four people had to accept job offers a month for me to hit my goal.

This means, knowing the rule of three in recruiting, I needed to get three candidates on an interview for one placement, which equals 12 candidates per month. From experience, I've learned that I need to get 10 candidates on the phone, to get one candidates to attend the interview. However, especially in today's text-friendly society, getting 10 strangers on the phone means I need to leave a lot of voicemails. Roughly, out of every ten dials, three would answer. Are you seeing how this works?

Putting this all together, I needed to make approximately 400 phone calls to speak with 120 qualified people a month, to get my four placements. This breaks down to approximately 20 dials a day. The only thing you can actually control in your world is the amount of cold calls you do. With enough small decisions that you can control, over time, you can have enough leverage to achieve your goal.

If my candidates didn't answer, I called somebody else in the database. I looked them up on Facebook to see who they were friends with. I called their friend and asked them if they happened to know any RNs in the Orlando, Florida area (but more on that later).

I kept track of my progress, my ratios, and my numbers. I ran with these numbers for 90 days. Why 90? Why not? Track your own progress and when you aren't on the path to your goals, you can analyze why. If you're dials are too low, you now know what you need to fix. If you're dialing more than anyone in your office but you aren't connecting with the right people, then you have bad leads. You aren't sourcing correctly. Maybe candidates are answering the phones but you can't get one to agree to an interview...this means you aren't pitching right, your voice isn't working, your tone isn't friendly or you're not coming off as competent. But now you know.

Utilize what you can control to get to what you need to have. Numbers don't lie. People do. Not necessarily intentionally, but several studies have shown that people tend to overestimate work they put in.

Cameron Morrissey shares, "I'm a big fan of writing out particular goals. I actively try to keep track of progress every year in August. From a personal standpoint, August represents the high point of my prior life. I was the director in a fortune 500 company. I had a wife and two kids. I was sipping on cognac and enjoying a Cuban cigar. One year later I was volunteering at a food bank, separated from my wife and kids." Reflecting on the drastic change only a year can make, he realized the importance of goal setting in his personal life as well as in his corporate life.

"I think it's important to mirror personal and professional as much as possible. Positive self-talk comes from looking at my goals and checking in every few months. I can track where I win in certain instances and where I don't win in others. I can identify history and find a trend of 'Hey I was able to get out of this situation, grow in my career, and even though there are doldrums, that's what happened in the big breakthrough.' I know if I keep working it, I have factual information that will lead me through it," Morrissey stated.

Brad Fowler, serial entrepreneur adds, "There was something that was instilled in me during my early years in athletics, as a young entrepreneur, and is an extremely integral part of all of my endeavors today. That aspect is planning. Even a small amount of planning can identify potential obstacles or flaws with your business. A huge part of the planning process is testing or 'practice' from the athletic side. Not to say that we get caught up in analysis paralysis, but in this day and age we have countless resources to plan, test and revise our strategies in order to work out some of the kinks before launching to the public. A small amount of planning can save thousands if not millions of dollars, which could be the difference between failure and success to the start-up business."

Chapter 6

# The Power of Forgetting Your Excuses

Shortly after being let go from my first real recruiting job, I sat in my bedroom reading and rereading the Merriam-Webster dictionary definition of disability. As I was leaving the office earlier that week, carrying a cardboard box with my belongings, my boss intercepted me. I remember him saying, "We love you but you need to take care of your health. Maybe you should look into filing for disability. Programs like that exist for people like you." Although my separation from the company was an amicable split, his words stung. "People like you". Who are people like me? What do we look like? What do we do? I looked behind me and noticed the wheelchair tucked into my closet. Solemnly, I thought to myself, "People like me have wheelchairs hidden like the depths of their souls, in their closets."

> Disability
> [dis-*uh*-bil'-i-tee], noun
> "A physical or mental condition that limits a person's movements, senses, or activities. Synonyms: handicap, incapacity, impairment, infirmity, defect, abnormality."

I felt myself nodding along, as my hands touched the page. I was the textbook example of impaired, defected, abnormal, and limited. This is what my former boss meant. I began to think up every excuse I ever had for why I wasn't entitled to the life I want. In an odd way, I felt myself becoming closer to my excuses than I did the people in my life. I started rationalizing with them, befriending them, sympathizing with them. My excuses and I became best friends as I read that definition over and over for what seemed like hours.

While sitting on my bed that day, I thought back to every poor decision I ever made in my life; from skipped workouts, to making poor food choices, to loving all the wrong men. Looking back, I realized that I had strong reasons for all of those.

Reading that definition, right there on that page, was justification that I no longer had to work out because I was physically impaired. I remembered back to when I was a kid in elementary school. I was playing with all of the kids at recess when the gym teacher blew the whistle to signal we would all get to run one mile around the playground. The fastest kids would surely finish first, earning another five minutes of recess which they would inevitably spend watching the slower ones struggle to make it to the end. I panicked on the inside and ran to the school nurse who immediately called my mom. I then played this wonderful drama over the phone where I begged her to not make me do it because I lied and swore I "wasn't feeling good." Ultimately, mom let me have my own decision and I sat watching the other kids run. My entire life, I never ran.

Right there, on that page, was justification that I no longer had to consider the dangers of what I ate and drank. After all, the diet encouraged in the Cystic Fibrosis world is one of high fat, high calorie foods. When I was in my early 20's, my girlfriends and I would all go out for dinner and they would order fresh caught salmon salads topped with strawberries and feta on a bed of spinach. Meanwhile, I would order the cheeseburger and fries, asking the waitress to add cheese and a regular coke. In my mind, I needed high fat, high calorie food, so I looked for ways to treat my body poorly. I clung to my excuse.

On that page, was justification that I was unlovable and wasn't worthy of ever settling down in a relationship. I thought back to my senior year in high school, when I was dating a guy I very much admired, who I left years later without any explanation. I told myself that despite the ring he put on my finger, he didn't really love me or want to spend a lifetime with me. I reasoned that if he did love me, he must be really mentally damaged because no real high-quality man would ever fall in love with a girl who has Cystic Fibrosis. I remember his best friend, a nurse, warning him about what it would mean to date me. I remember that for some reason he didn't care what she said. He would visit me during every hospitalization, and do all the things women wished men did for them. However, I started to find reasons to doubt his love and became consumed with the impossibility of it all. I let my excuses make the decision for me.

It's a funny little thing, but I let my excuses become my powers. That way, if I didn't feel like running, I had a perfectly crafted excuse to not push myself hard. If I ever felt like eating a greasy double cheeseburger with chocolate cake for dessert, I could just say it was because my diet requires it. If I ever had a fight with a boyfriend, it's because I am unlovable and I had an excuse to leave him. I told myself these lies over and over and I believed every single one of them.

A few years later, in the middle of a hot sticky summer in 2014, my parents were pushing me around in a wheelchair at Six Flags near Dallas, Texas. On that day I realized my excuses ran my life so much that I couldn't live. I was unable to walk far without choking on my phlegm. I was enjoying triple thick milkshakes for snacks, and I was single. My excuses were winning. And of course, it was all Cystic Fibrosis's fault, it wasn't mine. Or was it? As my dad pushed the wheelchair up the handicapped lane to the right of the rides entrance, I saw a girl about my age in short shorts and a string bikini looking at her boyfriend. I thought to myself, "Cystic Fibrosis ruined my chances of ever having that life." But, did it? Or was it all in my head?

Could it be that if I changed these things, I could change my life? Could it be that if I tried to work out, make healthy adaptations in my diet, and put my heart out there, my future could be entirely different? In order to take on the challenge of turning myself from a wheelchair, hospitalized Cystic Fibrosis and diabetic patient to a best-selling author and CEO of a successful recruiting company, I had to get extremely honest with myself.

On that day I started to become self-aware of the excuses I was making for myself. For example, at that time, I had another excuse I was hanging on to for not training hard at the gym. I used to tell myself that people were staring at me when I coughed. I rationalized that I couldn't push myself because of my health, and then I would wonder why my cough would progress. I wasn't able to cough up the extra thick, infection ridden mucous if I wasn't forcing myself to exercise. On top of that, fast food and canned ravioli for every meal certainly weren't giving me the energy to workout either. But were people really judging me? Was my coughing any worse than the grunts and groans people made while trying to lift their personal best weight for the eighth and final rep?

I had to tell myself things that I was afraid to admit. I was clinging to excuses like that and others, like the one that I had to eat McDonalds for lunch because I needed extra calories to maintain my weight. I had to come to terms that the choices, even as simple as what I was putting in my mouth, were affecting my health. Looking at my life from a different perspective, it came as no surprise that each hospitalization blood test resulted with me being malnourished. I was feeding myself, but I wasn't nourishing my body with nutrients and I was too lazy to start studying nutrition.

I was telling myself that I was unlovable because I didn't love myself. I didn't respect my body. How could I expect a man to love me when I hated myself?

On that day is when I decided that I would start running. At first I didn't know what I was running from, perhaps myself, but I started. I would spend my free time at the hospital running around the parking lot. I would cough until I puked, but I kept running. I ran from every fear I ever had, every reality that I was a leech on the system now. I ran from the reality that this disease has killed more friends than I can count. I ran from my choice to drop out of college, despite my 4.0 GPA, because I wouldn't live long enough to ever pay off my student loans. I ran from my failed recruiting career, feeling like I let my father down. I ran from every heartbreak, every man who ever admitted to me that he just wasn't cut out for hospital dates and weight-gainer shakes. I ran from the belief that my self-worth and self-esteem was unworthy of love ever again.

Until that day at Six Flags, I rationalized everything so well, that I believed my life was what happened to me instead of what I stood for. It was less than a year later, I was a certified Zumba instructor teaching all over San Diego, a certified personal trainer through NAS, I started a recruiting company, and had completed half of this book you are reading now. To add to the glory, I recently was in a bikini at SeaWorld with my boyfriend, kissing him while we waiting in line, interacting in the exact way I watched that couple at Six Flags.

We all have emotions and those emotions drive us. Think about a time you've had to bury a loved one...did you make any promises to yourself that day? Think about a time when you first told somebody you loved them. What did you tell yourself in your heart to make sure that you would never lose them? Emotions lead us on incredible paths but they can also limit us from ever reaching our destinations. We have insecurities that plague our day to day decisions. We have feelings that we are lacking in something, that we are inadequate. These feelings cause us to stay stagnant. It's comfortable to believe our excuses. We pretend we are happy as long as we have an excuse to cling to when we don't achieve a goal.

We all have unique circumstances but yet, we also all have similar excuses. If you are wondering what your excuses are, look for the statements you repeatedly tell yourself that surround the word, "enough". For example: I'm not educated enough, I am not healthy enough, I don't have enough money, or I don't have enough time. To help you overcome these common excuses, let me show you how a little bit of rational thinking can jolt you free from these binding thoughts.

## Education

According to a 2015 published census, 209.3 million people in the United States are 25 years or older, and 66.9 million of them have a bachelor's degree or higher (such as a master's, professional or doctoral degree). That means almost 70% of Americans do not have a four-year degree. More than two out of every three people are what some people would consider "under educated".

Many people mistakenly think they are not educated enough to be successful. They believe they can't possibly get started in business because they do not have a business degree. Or they believe that if they went to school but didn't graduate then they simply don't have what it takes.

Author and entrepreneur Sujan Patel states, "I grew up around small business owners and entrepreneurs. I'm a first generation Indian in America. My mom came here barely knowing English and started a daycare. She figured things out on her own and I learned from that. But fast forward to college and I was flunking out of school. I didn't think I'd get a job. I was kind of naive, so instead of continuing with college, I dropped out and started doing consulting work with search engine optimization. This gave me a taste of what it was like being an entrepreneur. It was hard earned money because there weren't a lot of opportunities and I knew I needed to continue learning more." He has now formed several companies including Single Grain, which has revenues over three million annually. Two of his other companies, ContentMarketer and Narrow.io are growing 20% month over month. In fact, he still doesn't have his degree.

Summarizing "100 Top Entrepreneurs who Succeeded Without A College Degree" by Paul Hudson (Elite Daily) the following is a list of highly influential and successful people who overcame lack of education to create something meaningful:

- Bob Proctor attended two months of high school and is now a motivational speaker, bestselling author, and co-founder of Life Success Publishing.
- Charles Culpeper, owner and CEO of Coca Cola, is a high school dropout
- David Geffen dropped out of college after one year and is now billionaire founder of Geffen Records and co-founder of DreamWorks.
- David Green never attended college and is now the billionaire founder of Hobby Lobby. He also overcame another excuse many people use, which is not having enough money. He started out with only $600.
- David Karp, founder of Tumblr, never attended college.
- DeWitt Wallace dropped out of college after one year. He went back later, to only drop out again. He since is the founder and publisher of Reader's Digest.
- Frederick Henry Royce, multimillionaire co-founder of Rolls-Royce, dropped out of elementary school.
- Hyman Golden dropped out of high school and co-founded Snapple.
- Jimmy Dean dropped out of high school at 16 and is the multimillionaire founder of Jimmy Dean Foods.

- Joyce C. Hall, founder of Hallmark, started selling greeting cards at 18. She never attended college.
- Kemmons Wilson, a high school dropout, is now a multimillionaire and the founder of Holiday Inn.
- Leandro Rizzuto dropped out of college and started a company with only $100, and is now the billionaire founder of Conair.
- Rachel Ray, Food Network cooking star, has no formal culinary arts training, nor did she attend college.
- Richard Branson, serial entrepreneur, dropped out of high school at age 16 and is the billionaire founder of Virgin Records and Virgin Atlantic Airways, just to name a few.
- Rush Limbaugh is a multi-millionaire radio talk show host who dropped out of college.
- S. Daniel Abraham never attended college but is the billionaire founder of Slim-Fast.
- Simon Cowell was a high school dropout. Now he is a famous TV producer of shows including American Idol, The X Factor, and Britain's Got Talent.
- W. Clement Stone, multimillionaire insurance man, author, founder of Success Magazine actually dropped out of elementary school. He later attended high school and graduated but never completed college.
- Walt Disney dropped out of high school at 16.

"Heading into college I dreamed of working on Broadway in production or management, so I studied theatre at Wayne State University and enjoyed most of those classes." Emily Schaller, founder and CEO of Rock CF, shares. "I began to stress out about having to take all of the other classes that weren't in my major because I thought 'why do I have to take these classes? Will I ever need this?' That mindset kind of spiraled my already non-enthusiastic position on higher education. This caused me to think that theatre wasn't my thing and that I just wasn't cut out or good enough to stay in and move to that next level. My parents were both teachers so I am sure they were thrilled when I mentioned that I wanted to take a hiatus from school. After a year and a half off, I returned to school for another semester or two. After that, I realized I was done. For me, and many other successful people I know, I believe that learning by doing and experience can be far more superior than a formal classroom education. So far, it is paying off."

## Health

Helen Keller was blind, deaf, and speechless, yet she was able to make her mark in history. Franklin Delano Roosevelt had polio and was still able to run for three terms during the biggest depression in American history. You can do anything if you put your mind and heart to it.

Every influential person I interviewed could agree that it's not what you have, but how you deal with what you have, that ultimately shape the life you build. We all have that one friend who we enjoy spending time with, but invariably shifts the conversation to their health and their struggles. They can drone on for hours about every medication they are taking, every doctor appointment they have, every option the doctors give them, and how they think or feel pertaining to all of these details and the correlations. Then again, nothing really sets them apart from the next person with a similar ailment. We all have health issues. We all have doctor's appointments that didn't go our way, or a loved one affected by a traumatic diagnosis. We all have stories of accidents, appointment scares, trials, and tribulations.

The thing is, if we are living, we are healthy enough to appreciate what we can do. If we are alive, we can dream. We can act. We can flourish. With certain health ailments, certain modifications might need to be made, but the excuse of bad health isn't really an excuse to stop pursuing your life. Sure, if you are in a wheelchair you may not actually be able to run. But if your dreams are to be as fit as possible while confined, you can definitely exercise your shoulders, biceps, and triceps. Aron Ralston is still an avid mountain climber, despite cutting off his own arm.

Influential people work with whatever they have. They accept the issue and leverage it, rather than downward spiral into the ever growing abyss of medical tests and doctor diagnoses.

The founder of IKEA, Ingvar Kamprad, is dyslexic. However, rather than let the diagnosis deter him, he decided to create Swedish-sounding names for all of the products so he wouldn't have to remember strings of letters and numbers. Even the name IKEA was selected based on an acronym of where he grew up.

Tommy Hilfiger once admitted, "I performed poorly at school, when I attended that is. I was perceived as stupid because of my dyslexia. I still have trouble reading. I have to concentrate very hard at going left to right, left to right; otherwise my eye just wanders to the bottom of the page." Nor is he the only famous CEO to overcome this affliction. Bill Hewlett and Steve Jobs both had dyslexia as well.

Rob Neville, founder of Savara Pharmaceuticals, had every excuse out there for why he wouldn't become successful, especially when he turned 40. "I had a severe health issue that caused partial paralysis from the neck down".

Fortunately, Rob had successfully sold a company prior, so he had some financial security. But he still felt as if his entire career he was climbing a ladder that was positioned against the wrong wall. He avidly went through the soul-searching process, which included a four-year seminary degree, volunteering, and even started a nonprofit with inner city kids. All of this was an attempt by him to figure out what the meaning of life really is.

Eventually he regained control of part of his body, but the other half still had intense pain that left him stranded to a walker. Determined not to let the best years of his life turn out like the current ones, he persevered through the pain and endured a year of physical therapy and running on the beach. Every day, tortuous movements kept his body agile enough and his mind stayed strong enough. He spent those beach workouts wondering, "What does this mean?", "What's happening to me?", "Why am I being put on this new path?" Not knowing if he would ever function again, he wondered, "How is this pointing me towards the rest of my life?"

He read all the books that his family and professionals recommended. He did all the worksheets he could find about soul-searching and mapping out his life. He wrote a personalized vision statement for himself, rationalizing that if he can create a vision for the companies he's run, why doesn't he have one for himself?

One day, during his workout, he was listening to a podcast that was featuring a woman from his homeland in South Africa. The lady mentioned she had four kids and one of them would die by that weekend of tuberculosis. Rob wondered, "Where is the world these days?" To know he was born and raised in South Africa, and here he was, feeling unfulfilled, listening to people struggle with real issues.

"It broke my heart and I decided to do something to make a real difference. I thought about tuberculosis as a lung disorder and how it is treated. It usually requires a specific cocktail of oral medication for a year, which systemically ruins them. Why not take a small amount of that and put it in the lung directly?" he thought. "I was able to write a vision statement for myself in that very moment. I'm a software engineer and never imagined I would be entering the life science industry. But I started investing my money into companies that were involved in drug delivery directly to the lungs."

Visions are usually described as big, audacious goals that may be unattainable in your lifetime. Goals however, are steps that are tangible, measurable, and move you towards that vision. It was that line of thinking that truly resonated with Rob. He realized that he could finally find something he could grab on to that would carry him through the triumphs and trials of life.

Once you have vision, things get very simple. If a company doesn't have vision, you get nowhere. Individuals rarely spend the time to figure out their own vision because most people are too preoccupied struggling day in and day out to take a step back and realize that the struggle is nothing without a vision. When you are down on your luck, when you are confined to a hospital bed (or in Rob's case, a walker) you are forced to think about, to take stock in, what you want to do with the rest of your life. When you have a vision for it, everything becomes much simpler.

If a spur of the moment project comes up and you can't decide between two options, you don't have your vision. A good vision will tell you if one of the options presented align with your project's goal. If it doesn't match up, don't say yes. Pursuing a misaligned project takes time away from your purpose. We have such a finite amount of life to live, why waste another minute putting out fires and accepting things that take the life away from your vision?

In Rob's vision, he never expected to end up working on drugs for the Cystic Fibrosis population, but he reflects, "I'm grateful for that and love what I'm doing, giving me insight into inhaled antibiotics, learning about it and wondering how to leverage it into the next big goal. I know I am heading in the right direction."

The process of developing pharmaceuticals is long. It is not the same type of adrenaline rush as climbing a mountain. It is mentally extremely difficult and requires millions (maybe even billions) of dollars in capital. There are many setbacks including the way patients respond, the chemistry involved, and the safety of the drug long term. Humans are complex enough, let alone creating a drug for them to feel better. Vision allows these small setbacks to come into perspective. Vision doesn't emotionally set you back because this is just a bump in the road of something that is ultimately meaningful. Vision allows you to maintain perspective.

"Your life is a story," he adds. "You get to write that story. You can run your life as though you're an actor or that you are the writer. So many people don't realize they are in control of where they're heading. A lot of people go through life, responding to life. But you should go through life like you are writing a story. Write a story that when finished, you enjoy being the main character."

## Time and Age

> *"I am not going to exploit my opponent's youth and inexperience." Ronald Reagan notably said, when debating for his second term for president. He was 69 when he was sworn in as President.*

We live in a world consumed by the concept of time. Many people over 50 believe they simply do not have enough time left to create a company, or to dedicate their lives to a new direction. In 2012, author Dane Stangler published "In Search of a Second Act: The Challenges and Advantages of Senior Entrepreneurship". Delving into the trends of entrepreneurship, the study found that in 2012, nearly a quarter of all new businesses were created by those between the ages of 55-64.

That is a 14% increase from 1996, according to Kauffman Index of Entrepreneurial Activity. In every year from 1996-2013, the study discovered that people in the 55-64 age range start companies at a much higher rate than those half their age.

There are countless theories as to why. Increasingly, older people search for additional income after layoffs or in the event that they realize their retirement income is insufficient. After 2008, many of the older generation who lost their retirement savings started companies in a field related to their career, thereby not only growing the economy but also paving the way for millennials.

There are actually more tech founders over 50 years old than under 30. Clearly, if age isn't a factor in starting a tech company, especially in today's fast-paced instant-gratification society, there is more to be said about the age bias.

Wally Blume spent 20 years in the dairy business and at the age of 62, after hearing his boss share an idea about tomato flavored dessert, decided to start his own ice cream company. He joined up with other partners and they experimented with several creations. He soon realized how delicious peanut butter and chocolate are together and Blume mortgaged his house to buy out his partners. He created Denali Flavors, the brand behind Moose Tracks. In licensing agreements alone, that company brings in over $80 million. "It doesn't take a Rhodes Scholar to understand chocolate fudge and peanut butter cups are going to outsell tomato ice cream every day of the year," Blume says in the International Review Minorities in Entrepreneurship, by Glenice J. Wood, Marilyn J. Davidson, and Sandra L. Fielden.

At 65 years old, after several failed ventures following a military career, Harlan Sanders wasn't quite sure what to do with his social security check. Check in hand, he founded KFC.

> *"You are never too old to set another goal or to dream a new dream." - C. S. Lewis, author*

## Finances

Growing up in Boston, Massachusetts, the son of first-generation Italian American's, Louis Spagnuolo wasn't born into a wealthy family. In fact, he was only eight years old when he had his first job, which was stealing food from the back of restaurants so his family wouldn't go hungry.

"It wasn't pleasurable. Success, in anything; business, marriage, family, it's about pain and pleasure. Most people base their decisions on avoiding pain or pursuing pleasure. I learned happiness is intrinsic. There was a lot of pain in being poor but even when I had only two outfits, I was happy. We were eating macaroni every night and chopped it into different shapes. We didn't have material things but we were always rich in love and support. There were never feelings of inadequacy. I had goals and ambitions, and was in awe of a lot around me. There was a lot of pain in being poor and that was my determination to strive towards pleasure." Louis shares. 30 years later he went on to become a millionaire entrepreneur and member of TIGER 21, an elite network of ultra high-net-worth investors.

Before he was 20, millionaire real estate mogul, Nick Ruiz, bought and flipped two houses, putting the down payments on his credit card. After successfully renting them out, he sold them, and made over $50,000. Within a few years, after repeating his business model with several properties, he was on the fast-track to financial freedom with a net worth of over $2 million.

Unfortunately, when the housing crisis of 2008 hit, Ruiz lost many properties and much of his income. Just a few years later he lost everything except for his house and car when he filed personal bankruptcy. For a few months he felt overwhelmed by his losses. "This was my lowest point because I was overleveraged and banks were after me. The market tanked and I lost 70-80% of the value of the homes. Bankruptcy was a way to free me of the shackles. Everyone around me thought it was unnecessary. They said I would ruin my credit and my business, but the smartest move I made was bankruptcy." Rather than accept defeat, he leveraged the lesson and realized that he had to begin again or risk never being successful. Fueled by love from his wife and daughters, he re-entered the real estate market through wholesaling, which requires much less capital and risk than flipping and avoids borrowing from the bank.

His wife and two daughters motivated him to keep going and make tough decisions that weren't necessarily the popular cry among his peers. According to his philosophy, the great thing about bankruptcy is there is no real penalty for it. "Your credit is screwed up a little bit, but it doesn't destroy credit as bad as it once did. Twenty years ago it was a big deal; now it really isn't. It's a tool of a smart entrepreneur. The most successful people in this world have filed bankruptcy."

It took a year, but his business was up and running again. Around 2013 he started a second venture, Alpha Home Flipping, where he offers online courses and one-on-one coaching to would-be entrepreneurs. "I never really made a whole lot of excuses, never had that in me. I was a salesman and entrepreneur before I was ten. This is what I wake up and do. I have a family and I'm an entrepreneur." Bankruptcy isn't an excuse to not reach for your dream, and Ruiz isn't alone in this philosophy.

Steve Mehr is an accomplished attorney and founder of business consultant company WebShark 360 says, "The number one obstacle of why people can't start a business is because they don't have enough resources, whether that is money, education, or connections. When they believe 'I can't start something' that is because they believe they are lacking something. But you don't need resources...you need to be resourceful. You need to problem solve and you need to do whatever it takes. You will never have enough knowledge, money, talent, and connections. I equate it as a good problem solver; I always tell people that if something isn't working, you just haven't figured out the combination of how you will figure it out."

"I never look at anything I've done as a failure. Not all my projects are working out, I just haven't figured out the variations of workflow or technique or the correct combination. Once I worked for three years, seven days a week, barely at minimum wage, and only saved $20k. But every month, every quarter, I kept rethinking advertising, operational costs, and that continuous attempt at trying different ways of doing the same thing. Eventually, I found a variation that does work and that's when most people stop."

"There are always obstacles. Nobody is going to write you a check. But the creativity behind how you solve a problem is resourcefulness. It's not a crime to file bankruptcy; go out and give it a shot," he shares.

> *"It matters not what someone is born, but what they grow to be." - Harry Potter and the Goblet of Fire by J.K. Rowling*

Travis Medley, the founder of recruiting firm, TalentZök, spent a little over eight years at staffing agency, Robert Half, when he decided it wasn't the right fit for him anymore. "The last thing on my mind was starting my own firm," he discloses. "I thought if I'm going to be in staffing, it'll be at Robert Half because they're fantastic." After submitting a four-month notice, he decided his ideal path would be to get a career as a vice president of operations with a smaller company but wasn't happy with the options that were available. "In retrospect, staffing was obviously the right thing to do. I decided to stay in San Diego but I didn't want to compete with Robert Half because they treated me well." He picked an industry he knew relatively nothing about because it had zero overlap in his previous career. With the guiding principle of "not keeping employees who weren't able to recruit as well as me," he ventured out.

"We went from no names in our database, to our first placement in five weeks." However, the success was short lived because Bear Stearns and the Lehman Brothers collapsed. Nobody was hiring, and it was as if somebody turned off the light switches for the economy." His new venture, his only option, was crashing around him. He completed only one meager placement in November and another in January. Until March, there were no placements, no income coming in, and no clients needing his services. "I thought I was going to lose everything. I don't know where we're going to live."

Even in his worst days, he knew in his heart he couldn't go back to Robert Half. He had nothing but a gut feeling that everything would happen for a reason. "I have my family at home. I had nothing else. I knew it could get bad and we wouldn't love our situation, but it never occurred to me that it wouldn't work. It was terrible for everybody, but it wasn't like I was sitting there wondering 'how did everyone else make it and I didn't?'"

The only thing that stops us from having what we want in life is the excuses we keep telling ourselves. Make yourself the promise to not simply go through the motions and blame your age, education, economy, or resources. We have our story of why things aren't how we want them and we hold on to that story and it stops us from moving forward," Medley shares.

In my conversations with Louis Spagnuolo, he shared, "Being poor is simply a state of mind. When I was poor I looked at it as more of a 'game' than as real life. My goal was to outsmart the game and do things to counteract whatever I may have lacked. Ironically this is how I got the nickname 'The King'. Every night for dinner we would have the same food. Pasta every night. But I decided that each meal I would be a King and come to the table imagining there being a meal prepared for a King. My family thought I was nuts, but the concept worked. I tricked my mind into believing this and carried it over to all other facets of my life. The key is you CAN'T live in reality. You have to escape from it and condition your mind to live in the world you choose, because the mind only knows what you feed into it."

## Fear Doesn't Exist

Atychiphobia is the fear of failure. And to some extent, we all have a component of it. But you need to realize that the only person that ultimately has any say in what your life becomes is you. That's right. You're in control of how you think, feel, and behave. At first, that can be terrifying. External circumstances come up and you have a split second chance to respond based on what you've conditioned yourself to do out of habit. You must empower yourself to believe that you can make the best of your situation and also have the perseverance to actually make that happen.

Sujan Patel reflects on his fear of heights, "I love learning and I learn best by doing. I discovered that out about myself really early on and wanted to learn more so I would do more. I was afraid of heights, so I tried skydiving."

*"He who has overcome his fears will truly be free."*
*- Aristotle, philosopher*

Facing fear is necessary for growth. Everything you have wanted is on the other side of your comfort zone. Molly Fletcher spent 20 years as one of the world's only female sports agents. CNN saluted her as the "female Jerry Maguire" as she recruited and represented Hall of Fame pitcher John Smotlz, PGA tour golfer Matt Kuchar, broadcaster Erin Andrews, and basketball championship coaches Tom Izzo and Doc Rivers. Successfully negotiating over $500 million in contracts, resulting in lasting relationships, she had the opportunity to learn and observe the traits of those at the top of their games.

As a public speaker, she specializes in helping people become the best versions of themselves as leaders, teammates, and sales people. "What if we replaced fear with curiosity?" she questions her audience. "I believe we all need to lean into fearful situations and embrace them. Usually, it's growth on the other end. That pit in your stomach, things that scare you, more than not, the other side is great stuff. What if we were all fearless?"

The co-founder of Netflix, Marc Randolph, shared, "'Risk', by definition, is trying something you don't know the outcome to. Failure isn't necessarily correlated to that. What's important is taking risks, and entrepreneurs need to take risks. People are successful because they tried things that were uncertain. Most people do not want to start something they can't see the end of." He goes on to share an example from his life. "I do a lot of climbing. One of my life passions is being outdoors. There is a progression of rock climbing. When you first start, you only want to climb things that you can climb down from. That way, if there's a mistake, you have an exit. But eventually you reach a point where you can continue to climb up, but you can't go down. Finally, you achieve a level where you can see the top of the cliff. You can't tell if you will finish, but you also know you can't really retreat, and there's where your highest risk is involved. That's a metaphor for business problem solving--small or large, taking a chance, even when you have no idea if your strategy is going to work. Start by making small incremental changes, then go all in."

Growing up, New York Times best-selling author, Austin Netzley, was primed for corporate America. Shortly after college he set out with his engineering degree, determined to be a CEO one day. "A few years in, I started reading and doing things outside the corporate world. I had a small seed planted in my mind that I could do more and it grew. I noticed there was a new world where I could create my own path without climbing a corporate ladder. "When he started seeing success in investing, he knew his time was winding down on his current career. "I knew my freedom was limited within the company. If you combine that feeling with the realization that I was restricted with my ideas, you can see why I made the decision to leave." However, with such a middle-class mindset, Netzley didn't know anything about entrepreneurship. He wanted complete financial freedom and to pay off debt, but there was an undeniably strong fear holding him back.

For him, failure was not committing. Netzley didn't believe in himself, nor did he believe in moving forward. He spent a year and a half in fear, dragging his feet and going through the emotions of that fear. "I'm very risk averse, and I would do things once they were finalized, rather than believing in myself and the decisions I was making. Initially I wanted to grow very slowly and organically because I needed a glimpse of hope. Looking back, I always pushed the gas pedal too slowly out of fear of going all in and failing, and embarrassing myself. It held me back every single step along the way. Transitioning from being less afraid and more of a leader, we were able to grow from a one-person shop to a 10-15 employee team." After success with his first book, he formed, Epic Book Launch, which puts together top-notch training and services to help self-published authors get their message into the hands of tens of thousands of people. He has created countless #1 bestsellers, including one book that reached #1 on all of Amazon.

> *"Believe in yourself, and the rest will fall into place. Have faith in your own abilities, work hard, and there is nothing you cannot accomplish." - Brad Henry, American politician*

One thing case study after case study shows is that in every situation, tragedy can be turned into triumph. It's simply a matter of knowing when your fears are guiding you, being able to recognize it, and move past that.

Some of us are more afraid than others. Whether it stemmed from bad breakups, bad business deals, or an unfortunate series of events, fear has a profound impact on our lives. If you let that develop over time without acknowledging it or dealing with it, small fears grow, become unmanageable, and turn into a guiding principle of how you run your day. This is how phobias form, rooted as a small fear that was allowed to fester over time.

Addressing what is holding you back is no easy task. Actively attempting to overcome fears is perhaps the toughest thing for people to overcome because fear is deeply rooted in our DNA. Fear becomes comfortable. It becomes a crutch to how we operate our daily lives. Fears, just like excuses, form our comfort zones. We rely on them to guide us in times of uncertainty. It's much easier to say "I'm afraid of commitment" in a relationship, than it is to acknowledge the love you have for another person might not be reciprocated. We can't be rejected if we are crutched into fear of committing. Of course, if you do not learn to confront this, your fear of commitment will lead to a reality of living alone.

Once you have the inner ability to welcome challenges that are targeted towards your fear and adapting an attitude of being proactive, positive behaviors will result. When you challenge the validity of security, your life can be reshaped. You will never have enough resources, you will always have excuses, and you will always be afraid...but own that. There is nothing in the world that can stop you, except yourself.

Chapter 7

# The Power
# of Forming Habits

*"We are what we repeatedly do." - Aristotle*

Over the years, I have developed a habit of taking my destiny in my own hands. I had to. I've been fortunate to have a great family, helpful friends, and incredible medical teams supporting me and teaching me, but I've also wanted to be responsible for what was happening to my body and in my life. Habits can be positive, right?

It was November of 2015, when my alarm clock went off at 3 a.m. My lung function was about 50% and I was on my third night of home IV antibiotics. "Do you need help, baby?" My boyfriend offered sleepily.

I kissed him on the forehead and said, "No, go back to sleep".

I quietly snuck into the kitchen, turned on the lights, and found my medicine pile that I set out the night before. With eyes still adjusting to the bright kitchen light, and a mind still half asleep, I poured the small cup of pills into the back of my throat and took a swig of water to wash them down. I trusted that everything is right because I knew that I had created the pile under a much better mental state. It is a habit I developed many years ago. I have learned the hard way what can go wrong when you try to count out similar looking pills with your eyes half closed and a mind still partially wondering if you are in real life or a dream.

Ever since I was a kid, strolling through the hospital after my parents went home, I had a fascination with all the wires that attached me to various machines. How do they work? How do I make them work? How can I rely on nurses less?

When a nurse first taught me how to turn off the alarm on the IV pump at seven years old, I knew there was simply more out there to self-care. I didn't think what I was doing was odd. I just thought all seven-year olds should know how to manage their own IV drip by starting, pausing, and disconnecting their own medications. We should know how to maneuver them while they are attached, because if we don't, how else can we use them as a skateboard and shoot the nurses with water out of a syringe?

After taking the pills, I grab my lunchbox sized kit of IV equipment and medicine from the cabinet, and wander over to the family room. The wire from my port dangles from my chest. I flip on the light switch and mentally make sure I didn't forget anything before I begin.

3:05 am.

Step 1: Remove all packaging on the syringes, IV antibiotic, saline, Heparin, and needles. Remove packaging from alcohol swabs and create a sterile field.

3:07 am.

Step 2: Draw syringe back 20 CCs and infuse the air filled syringe into sterile water. Pull back, drawing water out of cylindrical container and into syringe.

Step 3: Insert syringe of sterile water and air into IV antibiotic packet.

Step 4: Roll the antibiotic packet very gently to loosen up the mixture. It's okay if this one foams or turns yellow. Just don't shake it. Be patient.

3:15 am

Step 5: Repeat steps 2-4 with several more syringes to ensure a total of 2 grams of the mixture is in the final vial, ready for infusion.

Step 6: Inject slightly more air so mixture will filtrate out. Now you have 40 CCs of diluted antibiotic.

3:20 am

Step 7: Remove packaging on sodium chloride package and insert syringe into the 0.9% mix. One at a time, pump the diluted antibiotic mixtures from the syringes into the package.

Step 8: Attach a separate saline syringe onto Port-O-Cath (the port on my chest), and check for blood return, then "prime" the IV.

3:25 am

Step 9: Attach IV mixture to Port-O-Cath. Infuse 100 ML over 1 hour via guess and check method.

Step 10: While the IV is infusing, unwrap nebulizers including Pulmozyme, hypertonic saline, Albuterol, and antibiotic nebulizer.

Step 11: Begin each nebulized treatment, in correct order. Bring tissues and prepare for the coughing fit that will ensue.

4:00 am

Step 12: Check insulin levels with glucometer.

Step 13: Administer 1 unit of insulin, take hypothyroidism medication, take 6 digestive enzymes, eat a small breakfast containing up to 20 grams of fat.

4:30 am

Step 14: Disconnect yourself from your IV, flush your port-o-cath with saline and Heparin

Step 15: Repeat every 3-6 hours depending on the medications you have that day.

It's a pattern I know all too well. I've been repeating this for years, hundreds of days of my life, and haven't needed a home health nurse to help for as far back as I can remember. But now is not the time for reflection. In a few hours, I will need to be up again to repeat the cycle.

I crawl back in to bed, pull the covers to my side and feel his arm wrap around me. I gently squeeze it and kiss the back of his hand. I have a habit of living, accepting where I am right now. And right now, this is exactly where I love to be...in the arms of a man who squeezes me tight as I drift back to sleep, knowing I'm safely in his arms for another few hours.

> *"How you do anything, is how you do everything"* - T. *Harv Eker, author and motivational speaker*

## What Causes a Habit?

> *"A daily routine built on good habits is the difference that separates the most successful amongst us from everyone else."* - *Darren Hardy, author*

In recent studies, New York Times best-selling author, Charles Duhigg, explains that an estimated 40%-45% of our daily routines are from habit. Our subconscious mind is going through the motions and over time, the good and the bad habits show. We wake up, we brush our teeth, and we pour ourselves a cup of coffee. We have our morning routines before we get in our car and drive to work, all on autopilot. We probably spend the first part of our day checking emails and then reacting to what we read. At the end of the day, we drive home, past the same stores, on the same route, with the same traffic as the day before. It's a habit. We are driven to routine. People who are incredibly fit have a habit of working out and selecting healthy nutritious meals. People who run successful companies have a habit of waking up early and planning their day to be proactive instead of reactive to circumstances. Conversely, people who aren't in good shape have the bad habit of eating poorly. People who can't seem to hold a job have negative habits that have been stewing for years in their brain.

> *"Motivation is what gets you started, habit is what keeps you going." Jim Rohn, entrepreneur/author*

Habits consist of three parts. There is a cue, then the routine, then the reward. Think about what typically happens every afternoon at the office. One person begins to yawn, which is a contagious cue in itself. The person next to them announces, "Geez, I'm so tired, I've been working all morning and just had a giant lunch." The coworker one cubicle over hears, and realizes how tired she is. Getting up, she walks to the break room to make a pot of coffee for the office. The aroma signals it's break time, and a small crowd of employees gather to make small chat while they fix themselves a cup of java. A few times a week, due to a birthday party or awards contest, there is a box of cookies waiting to be opened next to the coffee. In thousands of offices across the world, this seemingly innocent activity occurs between 2-4 p.m. on most week days.

The cue, the yawn, is followed by the routine of meeting in the break room, finished by the reward of a caffeine jolt and mini-break during the day. This is merely a habit gone wrong. There are a considerable number of healthier alternatives to get an afternoon energy boost.

One coffee and one cookie, even just three times per week, translates into an added 26,000 calories a year or 7.42 pounds of added fat! It is estimated that around 60% of Americans are considered overweight or obese. All things considered, the sugar in the cookie and coffee every few days can dramatically increase the chances of becoming overweight/obese. In addition, our bodies now demand caffeine as if it is the only alternative to the mid-afternoon slump. In a matter of a few weeks, we have an unhealthy habit and addiction forming that is disguised as a treat and reward. Question where your life is headed, inquire within, change freely. For many people, a large cup of green tea can have just as much of a benefit as four ounces of coffee, for zero calories and zero guilt.

The habits you subconsciously have can set you up for success or destroy your life. The choices you make every day, lead to the future you will have. If you spend your day on autopilot, doing the same type of thing you did the day before, you will always be where you are now. In other words, you didn't come this far in life to only come this far.

It's interesting to inquire about the way our minds are conditioned. When negative things happen, do we instinctually blame ourselves? If our boss is upset, do we immediately think, "Well I probably missed a detail on that project so he/she is avoiding me?" If we are having a bad day, do we tell ourselves it's because we are insignificant and dumb? What is that tiny voice in our head always saying, always speaking about? If you're wondering what tiny voice I'm referring to, shut your eyes and be still. Soon, you will hear your own tiny voice and it isn't always offering encouraging loving words. Just like many are in the habit of eating cookies mid-afternoon, we can be in the habit of negative self-talk.

Alternatively, there seem to be people who in the afternoon are in the habit of a brisk walk and green tea. Instead of mindless office gossip, they spend five minutes doing a quick motivational meditation. Just as healthier options can be habitual, so can our thoughts. We can send our minds happy, positive, loving thoughts just as easily as we can send our minds self-sabotaging ones.

### Habits of Influential Entrepreneurs and Athletes

Author, Brian Tracy, notably said, "All habits are formed by habits." Every day, you should create a habit of writing out your plan with your top priorities and goals. In fact, stop for a second and think about what you can do right now, in this moment, to maximize the rest of your day. What about tomorrow? If you knew for a fact you had to leave for vacation in a few days, what would you do today to make sure you were prepared for a week away?

Martin Grunburg is a highly successful entrepreneur and the author of international best seller, The Habit Factor. In our interview he opened up about how he spent years of his life dedicated to the study of habit and the philosophies of Confucius, Aristotle, Ben Franklin and other notable influencers throughout history. Grunburg shares one of the key takeaways from his research, "We are all born and we are all going to die. We all eat, sleep, and procreate. Really, what separate us in our results, in our achievements, are our habits and our behaviors."

> *"All men's natures are alike; it's their habits that carry them far apart." - Confucius*
>
> *"It is very important that teachers should realize the importance of habit, and psychology helps us greatly at this point. We speak, it is true, of good habits and of bad habits; but, when people use the word "habit," in the majority of instances it is a bad habit which they have in mind. They talk of the smoking habit and the swearing habit and the drinking habit, but not of the abstention habit or the moderation habit or the courage habit. But the fact is that our virtues are habits as much as our vices. All our life, so far as it has definite form, is but a mass of habits, practical, emotional, and intellectual, systematically organized for our weal or woe, and bearing us irresistibly toward our destiny, whatever the latter may be. " - William James, <u>Talks to Teachers</u>, Harvard, 1892*

Grunburg further elaborates James' sentiments by explaining that both vices and virtues are essentially habits. A vice may be perceived as a negative habit, a virtue as a positive habit. A vice may be smoking or swearing; a virtue may be kissing your spouse every morning.

In my interviews with accomplished athletes and entrepreneurs, I asked them to share with me their top 10 habits; not knowing what vices or virtues they would openly admit to. Leaving the question completely open-ended, I was braced for the worst but kept my fingers crossed for the best. A pattern emerged. Five core habits came up over and over again. Ironic or not, none of the habits they shared were vices, but rather all were virtues. Every one of them took the approach that a habit is a fundamental association that could be used as a tool to kindle the fire of success.

## Habit #1: Going "All In"

Brad Fowler, serial entrepreneur, states, "One habit I've consistently had, was finding a will to win. When I wake up in the morning, whatever I'm doing, I'm making sure I'm doing it harder, faster, better than anybody would expect of me. That's the mindset that I have adopted. Going the extra mile is absolutely critical. In most jobs, people expect mediocrity. For an entrepreneur, you are required every day to give 1,000%. That is especially true during the startup phase, because you need to create more momentum and more buzz than anyone can possibly expect of you when resources are much lower. Excellence and outperforming expectations is a habit."

And Fowler isn't alone in his perception of the importance of finding a will to win. Boomer Esiason shared with me that having the internal fire to go all in was one of the key differentiating habits that he believed shaped his destiny. In every endeavor, he chooses to focus on that moment and surround himself with others that do as well. "There can't be a distraction; you can't take that day off, you can't miss this day, when you are successful and you meet those people who feel the same way, you know you're in it together."

As he was speaking, he reminded me very much of one of my own realizations. When you are fanatical about living, you can't make the mistake of taking a day off. Cystic Fibrosis doesn't take a day off, so I can't either. If I skip a treatment, I die earlier. My life depends on the habits I've formed to take care of my body through a combination of diet, exercise, and medications. At the core, there is no difference between the habits required to stay alive and the habits required to be awarded the NFL Most Valuable Player Award. When you habitually go all in, whatever your all in is, you surround yourself with like-minded, fanatical people, and you do not let distractions deter you from actions.

Boomer goes on to share, "There are a group of us that put on our show every single day and all of us have the same simple, yet clear feeling about what we're doing every moment. If one of us is sick or has something else going on, we never allow that to affect the overall success and momentum of the show. There are no addicts on the staff. We have an understanding of each other and an unselfish nature of doing our job to make all of our jobs a collective success."

Explaining further, he states that there are two professional sports teams (Patriots and the Spurs) that carry this same overall principle. "It's interesting, because when you put those athletes next to each other, there's true greatness with those two teams. And while they have superstars on those teams, they don't have LeBron James or Payton Manning."

"Tom Brady [the starting quarterback for the Patriots] wasn't the highest drafted player ever, but part of what makes him who he is, is he created an environment with his head coach to cultivate a 'singular of purpose' mentality." Esiason encourages all of us to ask yourselves if your team is all in, all together. Keep working and surrounding yourself with the right people until the answer to that is "yes". Then, once a team like that is created, cultivate it by making sure everyone carries out that mentality, even in the mundane tasks. Superstars that have an unprecedented run in greatness, do so in part because they believe deeply in that singular of purpose mentality.

Beth Sufian, prominent attorney and entrepreneur, shares, "I always try to do the best job I can do in whatever I am doing. If it's a case I am working on, I want to write the best legal brief I can. If you do your best, you won't have any regrets and you'll know you gave it your best shot. When I'm working a case, I don't leave any stone unturned. Knowing you tried your best, and gave it everything you could, is really a helpful habit."

When you go through intense situations, everything else becomes manageable. When you play full out repeatedly, your every action becomes all in. When you create a singularity of purpose on a team of like-minded achievers, there is no choice but to view the trials and tribulations as minor stepping stones. We all have massive talent; and some days we are just in that zone. When those days happen, take notice. Discover why. Leverage that new awareness to ignite your own internal fire on the days that you need a bit of a boost.

### Habit #2: Discipline

*"Discipline is the bridge between goals and accomplishment." Jim Rohn*

When speaking with Austin Netzley about the habits that led to his success in the world of self-publishing, he shares "The first word that comes to mind is discipline." Netzley spent the first part of his entrepreneurial endeavors living in a household with several other like-minded entrepreneurs. "We have entrepreneurs come to this house every day, and it just so happens, we move faster than anyone we meet. It is because of pure discipline." Every member of his household wakes up early, sticks to a schedule, and properly fuels their bodies with healthy foods and their minds with a constant stream of books. He admits that their lifestyle isn't easy. "There are always going to be days when the team prefers to sleep in, watch mindless television, and skip the workouts." But by holding each other accountable, they are able to overcome those desires. The reality is, much of his success he attributes to being disciplined about following the plan he created to get where he wants to go.

To become an expert in any field, repetition is crucial. Discipline is the pillar of repetition. People once thought that in order to be successful, you must be a "jack of all trades". However, with all trades literally being a click away, we are shifting to a culture where we want to partner with a master, not a jack.

Molly Fletcher, keynote speaker and sports agent, shared "I believe discipline is the key to success. I follow an early morning routine, and an evening routine." Everyone has hectic schedules, where everything in life can change in a moment. Our phones are constantly alerting us of news, emails, social media updates, competitor product launches, and advertisements...the list goes on. However, without clarity and discipline, you will spend your days trying to put out all of the noise rather than accomplishing what you want. You must be transparent with yourself about what is important. You must be transparent with yourself on what to say "yes" or to say "no" to. "Energy is my most valuable asset and getting clear on that is key. Having good organization is key." She believes that you must have anticipation for what happens in the following week. That way you can be prepared and maximize every conversation and situation you have planned. The intensity to perform is relied upon by the determination to stay disciplined.

Mastery is formed by intense repetition of a few core concepts. Think about how often Tiger Woods has practiced his swing, or how many times Stephen Curry has practiced a free throw. Think about what it means to practice something, the same thing, every day, for years on end without any guarantee of what the future could hold. It requires intense discipline.

Think about the last business book you read, or a seminar you attended. Or if this is your first professional book, think back to when you finished the first chapter. As you worked your way through the teachings, you undoubtedly felt a spark in your heart that propelled you to believe in the future, and of what possibilities you can create for yourself. It's amazing to me how many people will spend thousands of dollars on a seminar, to learn the "secrets" of success. They will get motivated, rush back to the office and eagerly start to implement some of the life changing ideas and concepts that they just learned. However, a month later they are right back to where they started because they lacked the needed discipline to continue implementing their new strategies. Ultimately they would have had more success if they opted to not go to the seminar versus spending the money on knowledge they never used.

Revolutionary new business ideas are in constant abundance. Life altering advice is presented to us daily. Choices are made all the time that dictate the path tomorrow will follow. Find a way to narrow them down to a few core concepts you want to focus on, and have the straight forward discipline to actually implement them.

## Habit #3: Early to Bed, Early to Rise

*"Mind over mattress."- Robin Sharma, author*

After a five-year study, Thomas Corley, author of *Rich Habits: The Daily Success Habits of Wealthy Individuals*, shares with readers that 44% of wealthy people wake up three hours before work starts, compared to just 3% of poor people.

In an issue of "Fast Company Magazine," several of today's most successful business leaders, from T-Mobile's John Legere to Chobani's Hamdi Ulukaya, were surveyed on their daily habits. Not one of them woke up later than 7 a.m. "I like to feel like I am ahead so I wake up very early," says Austin Netzley. "Usually by 10:30 a.m., I am completely finished with my day. The rest of it is just a bonus."

Other early risers include:
- Primco founder Bill Gross – 4:30 a.m.
- Apple's CEO Tim Cook – 4:30 a.m.
- Disney's CEO Rober Iger – 4:30 a.m.
- INVNT CEO Scott Cullather – 5:30 a.m.
- Tennis superstar Serena Williams – 6:00 a.m. She has stated that it is a "habit that started in childhood".

Nick Ruiz, millionaire real estate mogul, wakes up every morning at 6:30 a.m. "I like that nobody else is up; I get a lot of things accomplished with very few interruptions." In fact, when I asked the reasoning behind why so many successful people tend to wake up early, they state because the calm before the storm makes the storm much more bearable.

Rising early is a common trait for a variety of reasons, mainly because being the first one in the office allows for hours of uninterrupted time that can be utilized to work on the business, instead of putting out fires during the day. With lack of time being the number one complaint facing entrepreneurs today, waking up early has several other surprising benefits. There is a sense of control and power that can feed into the rest of the day when you have the discipline to wake up earlier than your friends and family. When you start the day proactively responding to an impulse that says, "stay in bed", you aren't giving yourself the mental satisfaction of being able to delay that snooze button and conquer your day.

Simply put, if one of your biggest complaints in life is lack of time...think about how much time that snooze button steals from your life. If you wake up an hour earlier every day, you would gain 15 more days in a year! Imagine what having an extra 15 days could do for you and your goals? Not only that, but knowing you started your day in control, as opposed to feeling guilty for hitting that snooze, puts you at a mental advantage to conquer whatever may come up. As you can see, there are very many good reasons that a majority of highly influential athletes and entrepreneurs begin their day before their peers.

## Habit #4: Living a Healthy Lifestyle

Entrepreneurs and athletes dedicate much of their waking hours to pursuing a healthy lifestyle. This includes reading, eating nutritious foods, and exercising.

Corley writes that 86% of wealthy people love to read, as opposed to only 26% of poor people. He found that rich people tend to read mostly nonfiction, usually self-improvement (books like the one you are reading now), and they read for a minimum of 30 minutes each day.

It's been stated on Entrepreneur.com that Mark Cuban insists on reading at least three hours a day. Bill Gates shares that part of his bedtime routine includes reading for at least an hour every night. J.K Rowling, the first ever billionaire author, recalls that as a child she read "anything I could get my hands on".

Don Langmo gives a lot of credit to his success to how much he reads. "I developed the habit of working hard, all day every day, and reading everything I could get my hands on. I've never met a successful entrepreneur who didn't read a lot of different things. You can only hear and see so much, but there's no limit on what you can read. [As a business owner] you have to have such a broad base of knowledge. You deal with finance, psychology, sales, marketing, organizational design, human resources...you must be able to read a lot."

Louis Spagnuolo, CEO for Don't Look Media LLC, reads for at least one hour every day. "Currently, I'm reading books from Joseph Murphy, and Napoleon Hill. I get lost in books; it's part of my nightly ritual. Anything I can do to learn more, to make me better, I'm attracted to."

We live in a world where we all basically have the same access to the same information. Never before, in the history of humankind, can a billionaire access the same files as a person living below the poverty line. One trip to the library or one scroll on a smart phone, can amass a tremendous amount of knowledge.

Netzley also shares, "When I was starting my first business, I was working a full-time job in the oil industry. Given a regular 40+ hours per week for my 'real' job combined with another 40+ on my side gig, I was overloaded. On top of this, I was a single 24-year old that was trying to fit in a personal life and travel, as well."

"I ate frozen pre-cooked foods from Costco to save as much time in my day for hustling. After a year of this, my body threw in the towel per say, and I had a few anxiety attacks. I had to call 911 multiple times because I couldn't breathe or fall asleep. Those were definitely some of the scariest moments of my life.

Prior to this I had played college football, ran marathons and was in seemingly perfect health. But, terrible food combined with little sleep and lots of stress on the body proved to be a recipe for disaster. After my second 911 call, I decided to turn things around. Now I eat high quality, healthy foods and it has made all of the difference in the world. My energy is consistently high and my focus is strong all day long. Just from having more energy and focus, I get WAY more done in my 40-hour work weeks now than I used to in my 80+ hour grind sessions."

Jeff Shelton, founder and CEO of Wholesale Warranties shares, "Every day, I make it a point to run four miles. Having ADD, I found that the run clears my mind after a long day and gives me the energy and vitality to push hard the next. Those runs are my personal time, my escape, and my inspiration. I live on a bay, so connecting with nature and reflecting on everything I am grateful for is a habit that I got into and I'm glad I stuck with."

Christina Waters, founder of Rare Science Inc., attributes much of her success to waking up at 5 a.m. and meditating, doing yoga, and mountain biking. "It's just you on the bike; you have complete responsibilities of your own actions."

Sharon Lechter, financial activist and philanthropist shared, "If I could go back in time, I would tell myself to take better care of myself. One of the biggest issues for all entrepreneurs, women especially, is that we put ourselves last. We take care of families, friends, business, and then ourselves. Part of my message now, is why I take better care of my health, and why everyone else should as well."

"Exercise helps clear your lungs and makes you feel better. Set yourself a target, even if it seems small. Once you have that, focus on trying to improve your distance or time. Make it a routine. Most of the time I exercise, it feels pretty hellish as I really push myself. A few minutes in though, it generally makes me feel better and my lungs feel clearer. I can accomplish my goals because of my dedication to exercise." - Nick Talbot, first Cystic Fibrosis athlete to climb Everest.

## Habit #5 Giving Back

> *"Your net worth to the world is usually determined by what remains after your bad habits are subtracted from your good ones." - Benjamin Franklin, Founding Father*

One of the things that continuously amazed me as I started to study influential people was their attitude towards giving back to the world to make it a better place to live in. Tom Corley found in his research that 73% of the 233 wealthy people he studied for five years volunteer five+ hours a month. This includes Bill Gates, Oprah Winfrey, Mark Zuckerberg, and countless others who all donate to different causes.

*"Strong people don't put others down, they lift them up."*
*- Michael Watson*

Every successful millionaire I interviewed believed very strongly that one of the best secrets of living a wealthy life is by giving to others. They create foundations they believe in and they donate their time and money to causes that mean the most to them, or have impacted them personally. From a young age, children realize that by sharing they get less. At recess, when the teacher tells them to share their snacks, their first reaction is to hold their snacks closer as a wave of sadness comes over them. They know that by giving food to their peers, they will not get it all to themselves. However, the influencers of today have discovered that by giving more, we get more in return. The more we do for others, the more we seem to get for ourselves.

There are several ways to give that don't require money. Time and opportunity are the only things in life that are not replaceable. From the moment we take our first breath, time is dwindling down. In a speech by Simon Sinek, he shares, "We value people more if they spend their time on us." Think about it...let's say you are celebrating your birthday. Two really great friends of yours decide to treat you on your special day. One friend gives you a gift card to your favorite store for a generous $3,000. Another friend, goes out with you to your birthday party, comes to your place a bit early to have a pre-birthday drink and catch up on what you've been up to since you've seen each other last. You two go out on the town and share a few laughs. A few weeks go by, and both friends suddenly need your help. Which one do you more instinctively want to help? Most people would say the friend who spent their time with you. You know that money is in abundance, there will always be ways to replace it. But the friend who gave you five hours on your birthday, they can never get their time back.

Martin Grunburg shares "I feel that if you can just help one person change their life, then your life is not in vain. For me, that is the idea of service. I am over the moon when I get a notification that someone posted a review of my app or book sharing 'this changed my life'. I never knew that's what I was craving or seeking for myself and it goes far beyond any dollar figure. One of the most rewarding things I've ever done is become a big brother through the Big Brothers Big Sisters Foundation. Some of these children do not have fathers. They need guidance in life, and a male figure that they can hang out with. Giving back is one of my greatest accomplishments."

Louis Spagnuolo enjoys giving back regularly. "Growing up, there was never anyone that would help me. I told myself, if I ever gained success or knowledge, I'd always want to help people that were below me." After years of being involved with structured philanthropic activities, he found that for himself, one of the best ways to give back was through shock philanthropy. Now, when he sees a kid selling candy bars to go on a school trip, he will ask how much he is trying to raise. Spagnuolo will then pay the entire amount. If he's at a restaurant and sees a mother with three kids, he will anonymously pay for the tab. "I've noticed the more people you are able to help, the more you receive in return."

Blake Cavignac, founder of Young Pro Elite takes a different view on what it means to give back. "For me, I never view success as an ultimate outcome. I think it comes down to identifying a need and focusing all of your energy and attention to serving something greater than yourself by constantly moving forward to helping others become more."

Every day it seems like there is a new YouTube clip that shows an act of kindness that can change someone's life forever. The person delivering this act seems to do so without hesitation and for no recognition. In that same day we may witness the opposite of this. Someone doing or saying something that only has their best interest at heart. Humans are at their best when they are doing things for others. "Some days I drop by my favorite bakery in Detroit and pick up muffins or cookies for the weekend; but on my drive home I may see a homeless person at the stop light and I'll pass that bag of treats that I've been craving out the window and let them indulge instead of me," Emily Schaller, Founder and CEO of Rock CF admits. "After Christmas is my favorite because I collect all of the uneaten cookies I can find and drive them around and give bags to all of my regulars on the Detroit streets. I love making people happy. Growing up my family got by but we did not live extravagantly. Weekend trips up north and lots of family time, my parents did whatever they could to make sure that we were able to do the things we wanted to do, but it was a struggle for them. On a personal level I try to give back as much as I can. I am not well off and basically live month to month, but that does not stop me from giving back every second of every day.

"Over the recent years I've adopted running and cycling as forms of treatment while waztching my lung function climb. With this in mind we worked to start the Rock CF Kicks Back program where we help others with CF experience these benefits. Kicks Back donates running shoes to people with CF to empower them to either continue on an existing routine, or inspire them to start exercising. We also register these participants for a running race of their choice. Maybe it's their first 5K or their second marathon. We just want to see more people move! So far we have hooked up over 300 people with CF with new kicks!" she enthusiastically shares.

Beth Sufian, founder of Sufian & Passamano L.L.P., has operated a legal hotline for 18 years which has provided legal information on the rights of people with Cystic Fibrosis to approximately 45,000 callers. "Many of the people have told us we have had a positive impact on their lives. That's certainly success to me. It is very rewarding to know you have made a difference in another person's life. It is unlike any other feeling you will experience."

Rob LaBreche is no stranger himself to giving back. "If I've learned anything over the years, I know if I make others better, then my situation becomes better. If you look at an individual, and if you can make their situation better, it will automatically open doors for you."

In fact, LaBreche started a charity in San Diego called Holding Hands. One year later, they created an event Heroes on the Harbor to honor wounded soldiers. "I still remember the day a friend brought me to visit wounded warriors in Camp Pendleton. Literally as I was driving away, I called the people managing the aircraft carrier USS Midway and told them I want to have an event there and rent the entire thing out. They agreed and for many years, we hosted an event where thousands of people showed up. We worked with wineries and bands and it was such a success, we were able to give back. In life, we are rewarded for serving others." It is through our own altruism, that our hearts are shaped.

Each influencer that I interviewed agreed that your life is a tool to help others. Ultimately, it isn't about the amount of money in the bank, how big your house is, or what vehicle you drive. Success is about sitting down at the end of the day and reflecting on if you were able to make at least one person's life better.

Chapter 8

# The Power of Sales

One morning, only a few weeks ago, I woke up in my usual hospital bed. "Good morning, Sunshine!" Robin Meade's voice booms through the television set. It's been a habit of mine to watch The Morning Express on the HLN Channel while in the hospital. I love that show... the interesting story lines, the entertaining side notes, my girl crush on Robin Meade. As I laid there watching Robin do her thing, my new nurse, Diana, walked in, introduced herself, then quickly made a beeline for the computer to scan in my next set of meds.

My favorite part of Morning Express with Robin Meade is when they show selfies that viewers sent in of their morning, wherever they are in the universe. You usually see pictures like a puppy sitting next to a cup of coffee, or a kitten poking its fuzzy head out from under big, fluffy bed covers. Sometimes the picture is of a baby wearing a funny t-shirt, or kids getting ready to climb on a school bus. In my head, I image a dedicated staff receiving hundreds of pictures every day from all over America. I see them looking at each one with a smile and deciding who will make it on to television that day. I'm not sure why, but deep down it's pretty radical to me. With that being said, two days ago I posted a selfie of my boyfriend and me watching Robin Meade, drinking lukewarm coffee, and sitting in this hospital bed. I guess they liked it, because I was about to get a quick little surprise.

"And this one comes in from Klyn, watching us while she's in the hospital. We sure hope you're feeling better!" Robin's voice said while my picture flashes on the screen.

Diana turned away from the computer monitor and exclaimed, "Did Robin Meade just wish you well?"

I sipped my coffee, beamed a smile, and jokingly said, "Well, since my last time here, I'm kind of a big media deal. Want an autograph?" We both chuckled. I said it jokingly, but I wasn't too terribly far from the truth.

"I heard the other nurses talking about that. You were on NBC Nightly News with Lester Holt, right?" She asked. Diana stopped what she was doing for a minute, and then continued "If you don't mind, could you tell me what it was like that day? I've never really met someone that's been on the national news before, and I heard what you did helped hundreds of people."

I smiled to myself. The look in her eye was so genuine that I couldn't help but oblige. "No problem. I guess I'll start from the beginning..."

"Back on my road trip to Utah during the summer of 2015, I made several wishes on the shooting stars I saw one night. Just before I got inside the RV, ready to go home, I saw one last meteorite. But rather than make a wish, I decided to save it for later. At the time, I thought I might need it if I wanted to take on the insurance and pharmaceutical companies to gain access to that lifesaving drug, Orkambi. Thank God I did, because it was about to be cashed in.

"Several months after that road trip I published a blog describing the events of that night. To my amazement, it went viral. Somehow news of it reached NBC, and soon after I got a call from the producers of

NBC Nightly News with Lester Holt asking if they could come do an interview with me. They had heard about the tremendous cost of Orkambi and wanted to highlight the struggle Cystic Fibrosis patients were going through just to gain access to it. This was my chance. I knew that if I could sell myself to the nation, I could pressure the insurance companies to change their mind, and in the process, save thousands of lives in addition to mine.

"The day that NBC came to see me at the hospital was numbing. You would think a day like that would be exhilarating, walking all over the hospital with a posse of a production crew, my best friends, and my boyfriend...But it wasn't. It was natural. To be honest, it just felt like I had more visitors that day than I normally would.

"The morning of my interview, my best friend came over just after breakfast with a dress and makeup. She spent a few hours with me making sure I was NBC camera-ready. My boyfriend took the day off and drove in to help me work through any last minute thoughts I wanted to convey. My parents called to tell me they were proud of me for what I was doing. I had the entire cystic fibrosis community rallying behind me thanks to Facebook posts and text messages. The nurses all kept finding reasons to "check on me" and see how I was doing. The hospital administrators called me to make sure I would respect the quiet hospital atmosphere the other patients needed and not say something on camera that would put them in a bad situation.

"The situation felt strangely natural. I was in the right place at the right time. I was ready to have a voice and to use my voice to speak for those who couldn't muster the words or the strength to do so. Since I was a child, I have given hundreds of speeches about life with

Cystic Fibrosis and how to thrive, not just survive. I have volunteered countless hours teaching other kids how to swallow their pills or telling parents that they should encourage their child to work out, despite their coughing fits. For over a decade, I have written blog after blog teaching both CF patients and their families that a meaningful life is possible despite having an expiration date looming over their head. Just because NBC Nightly News with Lester Holt would be filming and interviewing me in a few hours didn't make today any more or any less exciting. To me, each step I've taken in the last 28 years of patient advocacy was equally important.

"The crew added one final dust of powder to my face so I wouldn't look so oily on camera, then the lights were turned on. My IV pole was behind me, the cameraman from NBC was in front of me. Next to him, my boyfriend was sitting down, facing me and smiling with eyes full of encouragement.

"The next hour of questioning flew by in an instant. Time moved by faster than I ever imagined, yet slower than I ever anticipated. The production crew asked how living with CF affected my day to day life, how I felt when the insurance company denied me access to Orkambi due to the $259,000 a year price tag, and what I thought this situation meant for other CF patients and their families. They asked me how I felt about the drug company's CEO, knowing he makes several million dollars a year while thousands of patients die waiting for this drug. They asked about all of the paperwork I had to file to get compassionate use and discounts from the manufacturer. They pressed me to tell them the story of the drawn out battle I went through for six months which resulted in nothing more than a devastating paper trail and finger pointing from the biotech company, the research facilities, and the insurance company. They wanted to know who I thought was to blame, the insurance company or the biotech company.

"Mostly though, they wanted to know how an optimistic, energetic girl who does decline pushups in her hospital room, jogs in the parking lot, and has a reputation for turning the hospital hallways into agility ladder rope courses, slipped through the system and was being denied the chance to take a drug that could dramatically improve her life. They wanted to know, how somebody who has dedicated much of her life to helping others live, was just handed a metaphorical death sentence by an executive who decided her life wasn't worth the cost of the drug they created. How can somebody who does all the right things be denied the potentially right solution?

"And so I talked. I opened up. I shared how much I respect the right for a CEO to earn any salary amount the company feels they deserve, as long as the good they impose on the world is higher than what they are taking out of it. I explained to them why I push my body to physical limits; because you really never know what your limits are until you push them. I told them how satisfying it was helping others navigate the same problems I have dealt with. I even spoke about why I am so content with my life knowing that I could die in the next few years, but I feel the quality of the years I've lived by far exceeded the quantity. I just don't think a suit-wearing executive should have the right to deny somebody a longer or better quality of life because of profit margins someone calculated with the same surgical precision as doctor performing a lung transplant that I would receive should this drug not be approved or not work.

"After several statements like those above, the circus of lights, camera men, and production crew left and I went back to my usual hospital routine. Then, a few hours later, I got a call from one of NBC's producers. He told me that they contacted the insurance company and with one phone call, the paperwork was pushed through and I would receive the $259,000 drug that I had fought so hard for. Not only that, but they got a statement from the insurance company saying that in the future they would make Orkambi affordable for both me AND hundreds of other patients in my situation in California.

"An estimated 10 million people tuned in for my three minutes in the spotlight that night, which I watched from my hospital bed surrounded by friends and the love of my life. When it had finished airing, my parents called me and for the first time in my life, I heard my dad cry. My mom was full of hope that she wouldn't have to bury her baby girl. My support community of other Cystic Fibrosis patients cheered on the story, helping take it viral tweet by tweet and like by like. Friends I hadn't heard from in years, jumped on the bandwagon and relished in the change we were all capable of creating."

I finished my story just as Diana had finished hanging my next round of IVs. "That was amazing. I'll be back in a few hours to check on you. I have to say, you are really inspiring. If you ever need another person to help with your cause, I hope you think of me."

"Thanks. Yeah, I mean, it's all surreal when you're the face behind the movement." I added. "I never really woke up and thought to myself, 'I want Lester Holt to know my name and the drug company to give us all a chance to breathe again.' I'm not too sure how much of that I can take credit for, but I was definitely the spark for change."

"It's a shame how many patients I see losing their lives because of the cost of drugs. Just last week I had a patient that was so concerned with her medical debt that she would ask the doctors to run price checks on everything they used to help her. She couldn't even sleep; she was so worried about being billed for everything from antiseptic wipes to saline for her IV medications. Poor thing. You stood for change, you were hand-selected among thousands and you might have saved hundreds of lives because of what you did that day."

"Thanks!" I said. "I really appreciate that." All of a sudden Diana remembered she had other patients to attend to and with that, she left the room.

My eyes half-focused on Robin Meade while my mind started to reminisce about the camping trip to the Sequoia National Forest that my boyfriend and I went on just weeks before this most recent hospitalization. We went off-roading in his Hummer and I would squeal enthusiastically every time I saw a deer or a brown bear. We stood under trees that have been growing for an estimated 3,100 years, towering 275 feet above us, with trunks wider than his vehicle. We trekked my sore and achy lungs miles up and down trails, pretending we were the first people to ever discover this land. At one of the stops, we climbed 172 stairs to the base of one of the first fire-lookout towers built in the 1900's and marveled at the 360-degree view of the forest all around us.

That night, we camped under a starlit sky, where light pollution didn't exist and for the first time since our trip to Utah we remembered what it was truly like to experience a scintillating sky and the inspiration that only nature can provide.

Grabbing my hand while staring into our campfire flames, he asked, "Do you remember a year ago when we took the trip to Utah? I never would have guessed our lives would have turned out like this," he shared, his eyes beaming into mine.

"What do you mean by that?" I inquired, halfway fishing for compliments, halfway encouraging him to think about where we could be next year if he'd just propose already and let me live out the rest of my life in a fairytale that these forests inspire.

"Baby, in one year, we created a movement for patients. You still get fan mail every week because of it. Then, you started writing a book about what it takes to be influential (which I know is going to turn into a best-seller). Through our collaborations with entrepreneurs, we discovered how much of a need they have for recruiting strategies and implementation and we formed a company. You're my biggest hero."

Stunned, I sat in silence with the warmth of the fire comforting my face while the harsh cold swept around my body. Inside my heart, I had nothing to debate with him on that. All of that was true. I do get fan mail, I did start writing a book, and we do have a strong company dedicated to recruiting strategies for high-growth entrepreneurs. Outside, I still felt like my story wasn't powerful. In my mind I am just merely a human, in a sea of stars, in a sea of planets, in a sea of galaxies. The difference I've made isn't enough to change the world.

Sensing my calm, he asked, "What has inspired you the most on this vacation so far?"

I looked up at the night sky, then at the dancing

flames, then at the man who held the key to my heart. Immediately I knew the answer. One day earlier we hiked a little over two miles to one of only a few public caves in the area. After our 45-minute journey, we found ourselves at the entrance with a small group of people, listening to the guide tell us story after story about how this cave was discovered, the wildlife that visit it, and the enchantment of the people who were here centuries before us. Halfway through the tour, the cave opened up to a magnificent hollowed room that was carved out by centuries of glacial ice. Stalactites slowly inched down from the roof of the cave, creating a magical ambiance. A stream gently flowed around us. The sound of water was loud and chaotic, yet strangely calming at the same time. The formations on the walls glistened with calcium deposits, like glitter was thrown around by magical fairies for our amusement.

The tour guide, eager to show us what complete darkness was like, turned off all of the lights. There we were standing in the dark, imagining what it must have been like for the first people who discovered this place. Most of us had never experienced what it was like to be in the heart of a forest, hundreds of feet below the earth's surface, with no resources and no light. The only thing we had when all the power went out were our thoughts. We could choose to be afraid or we could choose to be inspired. After about 2 minutes, the guide flicked on her lighter and suddenly the inside of the cave was illuminated in the most fantastic way I could ever have imagined. The calcium deposits on the formations glittered brightly, lighting up the cave the way meteors lit up the night sky. The quiet babbling stream seemed to rush alive again. The thoughts that circled in our heads were calmed while our pulse was quickened once again

I AM ___ : The Untold Story of Success

with an intensity and fervor for our lives. It's amazing how much you can see with a tiny spark in complete blackness.

"It's amazing how much the tiny spark in all of us, can create a magnificent light that roars others to life in their moments of darkness." I said back to him, watching his face change suddenly as if I lit up part of his soul with my words.

My thoughts were interrupted as a text message beeped through my cell phone from my boyfriend, reading "I just saw you on the news again. You're always creating sparks, baby!"

> *"In life, you get what you negotiate, not what you deserve." - Dr. Chester Karrass, creator of Effective Negotiating seminars.*

Every one of us is born with the ability to become a great salesperson. On the day we were born, immediately following our first breath, each of us let out a gut-wrenching cry. We were cold, scared, and needed comfort. And guess what, it worked. Within minutes we were dried off, wrapped in a warm blanket, and handed over to a loving mother. Now some people view sales as the ability to talk unsuspecting people into things they don't actually need. But the truth is we all rely on sales to get ahead in life. Sometimes we use it to close a deal, but other times we use it to win arguments, teach others wisdom, and gain the trust of our peers. Learning how to be a good salesperson isn't just the key to selling a product, it's the key to selling ourselves.

Jeff Shelton, founder of Wholesale Warranties, shares the moment he discovered the importance of sales. "Back when I was 19 years old, during a summer break from college; I took a job working in the hot Minnesota sun doing manual labor for my family business. I wasn't making much money and frankly, I didn't have a clue what I was good at or where my life was going. A friend of mine recently took a job selling steak door-to-door. One day, he convinced me to hop in his truck with him and try it out.

"During my first hour I sold one of the boxes for like $180 dollars and I made $75 off that sale. By the end of the first day, I had already made over $500. That was more than I would have made in two weeks with the family business, without the manual labor or sweat. That day was the first time in my life I realized I was good at something, and that blew my mind. All I had to do was talk to people to find out if they wanted a delicious steak. It came so naturally to me that I didn't even know what I was doing right, and it was a heck of a lot better than sweating all day in the sun.

"This was back in 1997, and the steak management team told me that at the time, 5% of Americans were making over $100,000 a year. Of that 5%, 80% of those people were in sales. I was hooked. I know so many people that are smarter than me, more productive than me, or better business planners, but until you sell your product, none of that matters. That was the biggest and most influential part of my life."

Real estate investor, Nick Ruiz, shares a similar sentiment. "Successful sales people tend to all agree, when the economy is bad, those of us who are decisive and ready to take action can jump ahead. Why? Because a bad economy takes all of the flakes out of our industry. It leaves more business for us." He should know. The real estate tycoon started his career with nothing and was a millionaire by his mid-twenties. "Success is a psychology and anyone that tells you differently, is wrong. When I go to the grocery store to buy eggs, I don't spend time looking at them and laughing. However, if I go to the grocery store with a comedian to buy eggs, they probably will. Through their lens, everything can be hilarious. It's the same with viewing success." Ruiz's success came in large part to his sales ability. "Human persuasion is the number one skill for success in the planet."

When you lack sales ability, you lack the ability to be in business. Consider this for a moment. Everything you have in your life, you negotiated for in one way or another. Robert Kiyosaki, author of *Rich Dad, Poor Dad* admits in his book that he is not the best writer of all time. Despite this, his book has sold over 26 million copies and is one of the best selling personal finance books of all time. You can be the best technical author but unless you understand how to sell your ideas and leverage your resources to get others to want to purchase, your book doesn't stand a chance in today's market.

## Case Study of Sales Success

All successful people need to learn how to make a sale, whether it's selling your newest product, convincing your employees to go along with your latest marketing strategy, or even getting the coach to put you at the top of the depth chart. Sales are so crucial to success that practically every person I interviewed mentioned it at some point or another. Each one of them has a different history and strategy that works for them. To help you become a better salesperson, you should study the mentality of other people who have already succeeded in sales.

Don Langmo, owner of Healthcare Support and Healthcare Scouts, knows his recruiting firm would not be in existence if it weren't for his ability to identify and attract top tier sales professionals. "I think it's impossible to be an entrepreneur without sales ability. At some point your company will need to grow beyond one person which means you need to sell a bunch of people on the idea of joining your team." Unfortunately, when you are just starting out, no college graduates are knocking down your door for an interview. In the recruiting industry, if people don't know who you are, you aren't in business very long. Langmo elaborates, "You have to sell the vision of the company in order to find good people. The best candidates have a lot of options. You must share your dream and sell it. You won't attract and retain great people without selling your vision. In academia and at universities all over the world, 'sales' is almost a bad word. Think about it, no college has a degree in sales. They have degrees in organizational design and communications. But the truth is, 'sales' isn't a dirty word and nothing happens in life unless something is sold. "

Brad Fowler, serial entrepreneur shared, "Sales are about more than just making a profit. They validate what you are trying to do and they help you gain acceptance from the customer. Sales allow you to move forward financially. They are the lifeblood and heartbeat of any organization. The first thing they do is boost morale, they give you confidence. If somebody buys your product, suddenly everything moves forward."

The founder of iGrad, Rob Labreche shared, "Throughout my entire career I've been involved in sales in some way shape or form. Whatever job you're in, you will have a sales component. You need to bring your ideas to somebody. In a company, you are always selling ideas or the merits of an idea. Sales is more than just the vigor to work hard. It requires you to understand your audience and their needs, then work together to achieve what they are trying to accomplish. It encompasses my entire philosophy."

JD Davids, founder of Smart Money Startup shares, "When I started my own software company in 1998, I had a great idea. I put together an executive summary and plan. I went out and showed it to customers and received a good amount of interest. At that point, I began pitching the idea to investors, but realized I wasn't getting anybody to commit. One day, while talking to a business coach, a light bulb went off and I realized, I wasn't even asking for the sale. Later, I spoke with an angel investor, who I knew previously, and at the end of our discussion decided to ask for the order. I remembered asking, 'Would you be willing to be our lead off investor for $10,000?' You bet I was nervous, but I closed my first big sale that day. I ran into the living room, so excited, and so empowered that I realized all I had to do this entire time, was simply ask. From that initial investment, we did a billion dollars' worth of deals on a platform for clients. "

G.A. Bartick started his sales career at Nordstrom, selling lady shoes. "I was decent but not great," he shared. "I got myself into management, where for 11 years, I learned about the customer experience. I learned about what you must do to create a unique and positive buying experience for a customer. After that experience, I left and started selling real estate in Del Mar, California, where I failed miserably." After a slew of failed career attempts in sales, Bartick realized something, "Top performers don't wing it; they have a process. I met a Dale Carnegie executive mentor who taught me the value of processes. I joined him in a new endeavor that required me to work for him part-time during the day while still working at night as a mortgage banker. By 2000, I quit the mortgage banking business and joined Mike full-time. Seven years ago I was voted in as President." Still intrigued by sales and the sales processes that turned his life around, he authored *Silver Bullet Selling* based on interviews with 6,000 top performers and collected 33,000 pages of notes. "Top performers don't wing it," Bartick repeats. "They have a process." The rest of this chapter will highlight some of the most common sales techniques and processes you can leverage in your life.

## The Four Dimensions

Businesses can increase their profitability in one of two ways, either by decreasing expenses or by increasing income. While there are hundreds of ways to reduce expenses, the best way to increase income is to sell more. Many great authors have written books discussing this topic, and many of them are well worth the investment. Successful people make it a habit to never stop learning. But to get you started, here is a great overview of sales to help you start your journey.

Great salespeople understand that every sale has four dimensions; what is the buyer's want or need, how fast do they require it, how much do they trust the vendor, and finally, what cost are they willing to pay for it. Whether they realize it or not, every consumer balances these four dimensions every time they decide to make a purchase. For example, convenience stores and gas stations typically charge more for the same product than supermarkets because their consumers want their product fast. When you go on a cruise, you can usually buy a hand-painted plate from a local off the street for dirt cheap. In this situation, you are sacrificing trust in the vendor for price. Sure, the paint might smear off in your luggage before you get home, but if the price is low enough and the plate is pretty enough, we are willing to take that risk. The best salespeople understand these four dimensions and learn to leverage them against each other. Most of the time, we will never truly know how valuable each of those dimensions are to our consumers. However, the next few sections are going to walk you through the basics behind each one, and how you can overcome them.

The Want or Need

People purchase products or services because they have a want or need that isn't being fulfilled. A good product will sell itself based purely on its ability to satiate that need. However, sometimes people will genuinely believe they do not need your product. Many times this can be because they do not understand the value your product could give them.

Experts have estimated that in any open market, only 3% of the population is actively looking to purchase the good or service being sold. This is where the law of numbers comes into play. Good sales people know that in order to hit quotas they must talk with hundreds of people, relying on that 3% to actually say, "Yes!" The rest of the population is either not in their target market or not sure they want to be in the target market.

Great sales people, on the other hand, are constantly on the lookout for customers that are only saying they don't want something because they do not fully comprehend the value it will bring to their life. Another reason they might say no is because they hold a limited buying belief and think they are the type of person that will never want or need your service. For example, in my field as a recruiter, most companies I call don't want to do business with yet another recruiting agency. However, after I ask them key questions about their situation and share that our rates are significantly lower than our competitors, that want or need for our services quickly appears.

## Time

For many buyers, the closer they are to needing a product, the more they will pay. A sense of urgency is the biggest reason to make a quick fix purchase. Vending machines exploit this concept by placing their product directly where and when the consumer needs it the most. Every one of us at some point has begrudgingly spent $3 on a bottle of water or soda. On the other hand, when the timing isn't right, consumers will dramatically delay or alter their buying decision. When trying to persuade someone, remember that "A sense of urgency is the key to success. Everything now, nothing later." The closer to the timeline, the closer to the money.

## Trust

Once trust is gone, it can't be recreated. This is just as true in sales as it is in our personal lives. You can't and will never, get a good deal from somebody who isn't a good person. Customers are much more at ease and willing to do business when the company, the product, and the sales person all line up to their personal values. My dad is a sales guru in the office products industry. He is not the most technically savvy sales person. However, he does create instant likability with his customers. He has no problem convincing them why his company is the best to have a product from, why he's the guy to do business with, and why his product is worth investing in. In most cases, you can never fully experience the product/service before you make a decision, so you need to rely on the trust you have built, consciously or subconsciously, with the person selling it.

## Cost

Cost is surprisingly the one factor that is always brought up, but the easiest to overcome. If the price is too high for the customer, know that you are not effectively communicating the product's value, not showing them the speed you can deliver it by, or you haven't built up enough trust with them. On the flip side, if the price is too low then you could be leaving money on the table or worse, you risk them viewing your product as a lesser quality. To mitigate this, explain where the savings come from and how you choose to pass them on to the customer.

## Knowing the Right Questions to Ask

Understanding these four dimensions is critical to the selling process. Also critical, is understanding that each customer values these dimensions differently. So how do you know which dimensions are more or less important to your customer? The key is in the questions you ask.

In one of my favorite all-time sales books, *Spin Selling*, by Neil Rackham he outlines what questions to ask your customers to move them through the different stages of the buying process.

- **Situational Questions**

Situational questions are usually some of the first questions you should ask your buyer and they typically help uncover the context behind how they make decisions. These questions should not put the customer on the spot, but rather open friendly dialogue. Some examples might be, "What color scheme does your kitchen have right now?", "How does your office get its daily supply of water jugs?", or for my recruiting business "What kind of strategies do you use right now to find top talent?"

- **Problem Questions**

Problem questions are used to uncover difficulties or dissatisfaction with the way things are currently operating for your customer. These questions help them realize hidden needs by uncovering difficulties in their current method of operating. They consist of questions like, "Do you ever feel like your kitchen is outdated?", "Do employees ever complain about the taste of the water coming from the water coolers?" or "Do you have any problems with your current hiring system? How long does your current process take you? What is the turnover rate for the candidates you hire?"

- **Implication Questions**

Implication questions are utilized to take the problem you uncovered and make the customer think about dire consequences of not solving that problem. It also makes the customer realize the problem went from being only trivial to potentially very damaging for them, should it go unaddressed. For example, "Do you ever feel like people are judging you when they see your kitchen?", "Have clients ever gotten a bad impression of your company because the water cooler was empty or was an off-brand?", or "If it takes that long to hire a sales candidate, how does that affect your staff? Sales performance? What is the ramp up period? Is the high turnover creating negative buzz about your company to potential buyers or other candidates?"

- **Need-Payoff Questions**

Need-payoff questions are utilized to ask the importance of the solution your unique product/service offers. These types of questions usually give your customer a sigh of relief as they invoke positive feelings, usefulness, and a constructive solution to a mounting problem. "Would you be more excited to host social functions if you had a new kitchen?", "Do you think your employees would feel more appreciated if they had better quality water coolers?", or "Would it be useful if we did a four-hour corporate training workshop on the strategies we use to hire top talent, in under 21 days, for virtually any position?"

In an interview I conducted with Jason Forrest, author and sales training guru, he offered up the five core concepts he teaches in his seminars. "Every building has a sturdy foundation at the bottom. That foundation is the definition of leader. A great sales person is a great leader. A leader is a person you follow to a place that you're not willing to go. Most people think it's only a high title, but I believe that everyone has a leader within them that must be unleashed. We want sales people to be leaders, because customers want to be lead."

"The first pillar is the definition of selling; giving certainty plus education with rapport to another human being. The concept is very simple, customers need certainty to buy. Think about it. If a person is already 100% certain, then they don't need a sales person. I recently went to Amazon and bought a camera. I already knew what brand I wanted. I had already been sold. I just did it. I didn't talk to a sales person; I already had certainty. I was already educated on the product and the value of this camera. Often sales people think, 'If I get more interested customers, I'll do better'. But that's not necessarily true. A salesperson's job is to make a customer more certain by giving them education with rapport. It's not about getting them to like you; it's about earning their respect. Customers want a leader and a business advisor relationship more than anything else. You don't need to be their friend to be even friendly for that matter. My definition of rapport is mutual purpose and mutual respect. If you create that, you will have more rapport."

"The second pillar is the purpose of selling. The purpose of this pillar is to convince the 'just looking' buyer to buy from you today over all alternatives. What do you think your purpose is? Often times, sales professionals are told to educate, guide, and instruct. That's what you do, but your purpose is to convince your buyer to buy today, over all alternatives. Most customers don't come back for a second visit. If they don't buy from you, where are they going to spend their money? They may do it on a car, vacation, clothing, anything but your product. You only have today."

"The third pillar is the rule of selling in which you make it easy for customers to give you their money. Most of the time we make things too complicated by having too many choices. For example, look at Apple. They only have a handful of products. Look at In-N-Out Burger, there's less than a handful of lunch options. How can the most profitable stores have half as many options? Customers want simplicity. "

"Lastly, the fourth pillar is the objective of selling. Your main objective is to lead the customer towards making decisions that achieve their resolution and make them feel completely confident that the decision they made was right. When it comes to buying, there are always many decisions. Resolution is important because the most crippling disease is ambiguity. Should I go to college? Get married? Get divorced? Customers don't want another to do item. They want to get to a point of resolution and to secondly, make them feel wanted. If they feel big, they buy big. If they feel small, buy small."

Once you change your viewpoints on selling, you will discover that it is one of the noblest professions that exist. Great sales people have the ability to lead people and influence them towards making a life-changing and life-improving decision. They empower not only their own life, but the lives of the people they influence. It's not simply about making somebody buy something. Selling requires a certain mindset and mental toughness, beliefs, and thought patterns that push people to become better versions of themselves or lead better versions of their teams, company, and relationships.

Molly Fletcher, hailed by CNN as the "female Jerry Maguire", shares "What I learned from my first job answering phones at the Superbowl as part of the Super Bowl host committee, is when we work with people, we become an extension of one another. Later in life, as one of the first female sports agent's, I had so much appreciation and gratitude for being an extension of my players. I never took for granted the value they placed on me being associated with their name. When I was on the phone representing John Smoltz, I was the extension of a terrific human being. Handling those calls in the right way was incredibly important. As a speaker, when an executive has the courage to put me on a stage in front of their most important group, their employees, my ability to have a positive extension of them is of upmost importance. I think relationships are the anchor to our business success. So to me, it's about giving, and giving, and giving, and building. You need to build favors with people you want to work with. It is about creating a platform that allows the people you're selling to experience the relationship you are creating. Before you buy a car, you take a test drive. In much the same way, people want to test drive a business relationship. I would recruit athletes and act like I represent them before I did. Often act like you have the business before you have the business."

I remember the day when I first met my better half outside of a classy restaurant in San Diego. I had backup plans that night, just in case he turned out to be a dud, but

I decided to cancel them in the first five seconds based on the way he flashed his smile and brought energy into the room that matched the energy of the butterflies in my stomach. He didn't say anything mind-blowing that evening over dinner. He didn't particularly seem like the most educated, wealthy, or best-dressed man in the restaurant. However, he did speak with an air of confidence and gave me the impression that should I choose to spend my time with him, my life would be significantly better than if I picked any other man on this planet.

As a blonde living in paradise, I definitely had my pick of dates. There was something about him though. He sold me. He put his best self forward and learned about my life, asking great questions to uncover who I was as a human, and illustrated to me that I could be whoever I wanted to be, if I just managed to have one more drink with him. One more date. One more walk up the boardwalk. I learned that night, if you can sell a blonde in paradise on a second date, you can sell anything.

And whether you are getting your story featured on national news to save lives, selling your training systems, recruiting sports professionals, or convincing a hot blonde to sit at your side at a bar, at the end of the day success comes from being a fantastic human being who puts other people's interests above your own. If you can persuade someone in an ethical manner to see how your product or message or vision relates to an improvement in their life, you can do anything. In our lives, we are either being sold something or selling something at every moment of every day. You need to pick what side you want to be on.

Chapter 9

# The Power of
# Living Wonderfully

I glanced down at the sheet of paper my respiratory therapist had printed out just moments ago before leaving the room. The date marked on the upper left side, my name and patient ID# typed in the middle, and the numbers of my lung function for the past year. I glanced at the declining numbers in partial disbelief, the way a student looks at their score after failing a test, or an athlete looks at the scoreboard following a horrible performance.

My boyfriend squeezed my hand, tears welling in his eyes. He looked away from me, lips pursed, jaw jutting out, eyes darting across the hospital room. His gaze landed on the stethoscope, hanging from the wall to his left. He squeezed my hand harder. "What...what does this mean?" his voice trembling.

It's been almost eight months since Orkambi was delivered from the pharmacy to my doorstep. During that time, I was able to hit new personal records at the gym, run farther than I ever have before, and breathe deeper than I ever thought possible. Currently, as I write this, I am sitting in my all too familiar hospital bed on the 2nd floor of the UCSD Hospital in La Jolla, California. This is my second hospitalization since I started on the drug that I had put so much energy into obtaining, all the while hoping it would stabilize my lungs long enough for me to see another decade. On the first hospitalization, I rationalized that I caused it myself by forgetting to take my digestive enzymes, resulting in nutritional deficiencies that caused my lungs to flare up. I would rather believe it was my fault than confront the reality that maybe Orkambi wasn't working for me.

The side effects the first few months since receiving the drug were rather intense. Some days it would feel as if an elephant was sitting on my chest. Other days I would cry for no reason. My hair started to fall out, at first a few strands and more recently, in clumps. I found myself dizzy quite often and my vision seemed to be slightly worsening. After workouts, I became accustomed to chugging electrolyte water to combat the intense dehydration that would happen due to the imbalance of sodium in my body. My boyfriend and I were warned that my birth control would no longer work, and had talked about our intentions to have a family or not. The list of side effects on the medical pamphlets was dizzying in itself, but we argued that it was worth every side effect if I lived longer. Despite these inconveniences, I told myself every day that I was healthy and the drug was working...because in my mind...it was my hope. It was my lifeline.

"This means we enjoy our lives together." I said trying to keep my own voice firm but encouraging. I kissed the top of his hand.

"But," he pleaded. "I thought you were going to be fine. How is your lung function back at 57%? I thought this was the miracle that would keep you from dying so young." He let go of my hand and walked across the room to stare out of my window.

His palms and forehead touched the glass and in his reflection, I saw a tear leaving his eyes. A year of heartbreak and a lifetime of shattered hope, escaping through his eyes, reflected back at me from the window pane. It's the strangest thing to see one of the toughest men you know lose his strength. He gently tapped the window with his forehead and clenched his fists, ready to pound the glass.

I stood up, walked over, and put my arms around his waist. Then I kissed the back of his shoulders. "My darling, nothing has changed. My lungs are weaker, yes, but I'm going back on IV's, and my life is too important to stop living it now. We can still have our dreams, baby. We're still going to do this together." He shrugged as his fists left the window pane to wipe his face and turn toward me. Avoiding eye contact, he kissed my forehead and wrapped his arms around my waist. He rested his chin on my head and took a deep breath.

There really are no words of encouragement you can give your partner in times like this. There is nothing I can say, nothing to express. Even the lies I tell myself about how strong I am, feel empty yet heavily weighted.

I let the warmth of his body comfort me as I choke back my own tears. It's hard enough to look at a list from the past year of declining lung function and accepting that no matter what you do, time may be running out. But it's even harder to accept those numbers when you had such high hope that the time wouldn't run out so quickly because you fought for a prescription drug that would halt that progression.

"You know what this reminds me of?" He offers. "In college I took a history class and we studied torture. There's this thing they do to prisoners, where they lock them in a cell and put food on the other side of the bars. The captive is forced to stare at the food, while they slowly starve to death. There's hope that they will live but day after day, they waste away and the guards won't do a thing to stop it because somebody else controls their actions. They gave you a bite finally, but it's not enough to keep you alive and you're still running on only hope that tomorrow there will be something of substance."

"Please, sit by me," I asked, walking away from the window to my hospital bed. He shrugged and walked over.

"I don't want to live a moment without you in my life." He said forcing back more tears.

"So don't." I shot him a wide-eyed, love me forever type of smile. I laugh to myself thinking any second he may propose, as if that's going to cure my lungs. My heart maybe, but not my lungs.

"What can we do now?" He asked.

"The way I see it, we keep going. We show the world what we can do with half of a functioning lung, while we go back on antibiotics to regain some of what the infection is taking. We take no excuses and we give no apologies for living freely. We use our voices instead of hiding behind the veil that everything is okay."

"What do you want to do with your life, Klyn?"

"What the world doesn't need is another pity party or the tragic death of somebody who never lived." I started. "I want to continue to build out my recruiting company, start a corporate talent strategy and acquisition side to the business."

"Let's do it. Your employees can all work remotely. Without the overhead, we can pass the savings on to the clients and because you don't have a traditional office, you can work from home or this place. We can even donate a portion of the profits to that charity that supports athletes with CF. What else do you want?"

"I want to finish my book and continue to make friends with powerful entrepreneurs."

"We can do that, too." He replied instantly.

"What about you, babe?" I asked. "What would you do today if you knew you had absolutely nothing to lose?"

"I want to grow my company to surpass the $10 million in revenue mark," he offered. "I believe we can and I think I have been playing to keep, not necessarily to win. I want to win." It's amazing how much ambition was in the room, despite the grave circumstances. "There's one more thing though, I also want to spend every moment and dedicate the rest of my life to being by your side."

"You know Klyn, I am thankful for your torture, without it, we have nothing." He went on to say. "I don't think I've ever been able to appreciate the moments I have in life. I don't think I ever really thought about how to grow and live in the moment the way you do."

I smiled back at him, and remembered the quote about how too many people quit living at 25 but don't die until they are in their 80's. Sometimes it's easy to give out advice, or listen to others give it to you. But when adversity rears its head, we revert back to our comfort zones. My struggle might be tough, but is it really any different than the same ones so many entrepreneurs and athletes have faced?

I thought back to the countless stories I learned from my interviews. I put myself in Boomer Esiason's shoes when he first looked at the University of Maryland's depth chart and saw his name as the 11th quarterback. I'm sure he was looking at that number the same way I looked at my lung function chart a few hours ago.

I thought back to the pain Larry Linne must have felt after suffering that monstrous crash. What was it like laying on the ground with a separated shoulder, broken collarbone, broken elbow, and three broken bones in his hand? Was that so much different than the pain I've felt when I had my coughing spells and starting coughing blood? Or how did he feel crossing the finish line of the Leadville Trail 100 MTB only three weeks later? Could I possibly feel that way someday when I'm about to step on stage as an award-winning author, CEO, and motivational speaker?

JV Crum III spent part of his life with a $5/week budget for food. Rob LaBreche was fired from his job the day after his wedding. Andre' Phillipe van den Broeck fell into a life of drugs and fights after his parents divorced, only to turn his life around, forming a highly successful company, then watch it crash again with eviction notices, repossessed cars, and no way to feed his dog. Louis Spagnuolo found a way to build an empire, even when all he had as a child was poverty and pasta. Jeff Shelton found a way to abandon his family business and take a risk by moving to San Diego with nothing, to wind up in a hospital room with the love of his life and a $7 million in revenue company. They all found ways to overcome their lowest moments, and so can I.

Just then my inner motivational speech was broken. "I love you, Klyn Elsbury." He said.

"I love you too, Jeff Shelton."

And so the story goes. I finished writing this book while on another round of IV antibiotics, from the comforts of a 24-7 drip, staring out the same window Jeff beat his palms against in emotional agony. He would spend nights with me at the hospital and during the day, he implemented new programs for his customers to benefit from at Wholesale Warranties. In between treatments, I hired four remote employees and my team placed 11 candidates during this hospitalization, finishing our strongest month on record for the company I formed, Landmark Makers. I booked a dozen speaking engagements and podcasts, shooting my voice to thousands of people about how wonderful our lives really are. I'm still wildly optimistic that one day, the fourth wish I made on the rooftop of his RV will have come true but in the meantime, I will not stop living every single day to its absolute fullest.

# Glossary of Key Influencers and their Chapters of Contribution

## G.A. Bartick – Ch. 8

G.A. Bartick is a national speaker and facilitator at conventions and meetings around the world. He has been in sales his entire career and uses his experience, knowledge, enthusiasm and personal style to connect with his audience and inspire improved performance.

G.A. has also implemented hundreds of consultative sales and customer service programs for clients such as Google, Cox Communications, Time Warner, City National Bank, Merrill Lynch, MetLife, Morgan Stanley and Expedia.com. One of his passions is one-on-one coaching with senior executives and managers. In all, G.A. is on the road at least 40 weeks a year transferring his knowledge and enthusiasm to leadership, sales and customer service professionals. He is also the author of national bestseller, *Silver Bullet Selling: Six Critical Steps to Opening More Relationships and Closing More Sales* which is published by John Wiley & Sons.

## J.V. Crum III – Ch. 4, 5

J V Crum III helps established business owners and coaches build companies that make a big impact and big profits. He is the Founder and CEO of ConsciousMillionaire.com, that provides training, coaching, and masterminds through its First Million Academy. J V is a speaker, coach, Huffington Post Columnist, and #1 best-selling author of *Conscious Millionaire: Grow Your Business by Making a Difference*. He hosts the top-ranked "Conscious Millionaire Show & Podcast" and holds an

MBA, JD, and Masters in Psychology. J V has built and sold successful companies, and is featured in the upcoming movie, RiseUP.

## Blake Cavignac – Ch. 1, 2, 4, 7

Blake Cavignac is the Founder of YoungPro Elite. Over the past ten years he has had the privilege of leading thousands of college students and young professionals through his companies and the programs he has created. Due to this experience, prominent organizations are now calling on Blake to solve one of their biggest challenges: attracting, developing and retaining the top young talent in their industry.

According to Ben Drake, "Blake is one of those dynamic individuals you read about in leadership books that you hope to work for." The president of HNI, Mike Natalizio says, "Whether you're a young professional or a seasoned professional, you should follow Blake and the trail he's blazing."

Recognized as the leader of young leaders, executives and professionals come to Blake and his team at YoungPro Elite when they need solutions relating to leadership and development of young talent.

## J.D. Davids – Ch. 2, 8

J.D. is one of the most accomplished startup dealmakers in the world. He has completed well over $1 Billion in financial transactions over the last 25 years. J.D. has served on the management teams of eight venture capital-backed startups and three of those companies completed successful initial public offering (IPO's), and three of them were acquired by large corporations. Prior to his work with startups, J.D. served four years of active duty in the United States Marine Corps.

At this point in his career, J.D. has dedicated his life to helping thousands of entrepreneurs raise money, build great companies, and close exit events that generate huge financial returns. Companies that work closely with J.D. experience a transformation from being merely good entrepreneurs into some of the most savvy strategic dealmakers in the startup ecosystem today.

## Boomer Esiason – Ch. 2, 4, 7

Boomer Esiason is a former NFL quarterback and sports commentator. He was born and raised in East Islip, New York and played college football for the University of Maryland. Boomer was selected by the Cincinnati Bengals in the second round of the NFL draft where he became a starting quarterback for several years before also playing for the New York Jets and Arizona Cardinals.

During his career in the NFL, he was selected for four pro-bowls, led the AFC in passing yards twice, and won the NFL Most Valuable Player Award in 1988.

Following his football career, he worked as a broadcast commentator for ABC's *Monday night Football* and then became an analyst for *The NFL Today* on CBS. He currently hosts "Boomer and Carton" in the morning for WFAN radio in New York and the CBS Sports Network.

After finding out his son has Cystic Fibrosis, Boomer founded the Boomer Esiason Foundation to support hospitals in the treatment of CF and provide scholarship grants to CF patients.

## Molly Fletcher – Ch. 6, 7, 8

Molly Fletcher is a trailblazer in every sense of the word. She is a rare talent of business wisdom, relationship brilliance and unwavering optimism. As a CEO, she shares her unconventional and unique techniques that made her one of the first female sports agents in the high stakes, big ego world of professional sports and now a successful entrepreneur. As president of client representation for sports and entertainment agency CSE, Molly spent two decades as one of the world's only female sports agents. She was hailed as the "female Jerry Maguire" by CNN as she recruited and represented hundreds of sport's biggest names, including Hall of Fame pitcher John Smoltz, PGA TOUR golfer Matt Kuchar, broadcaster Erin Andrews, and basketball championship coaches Tom Izzo and Doc Rivers. As she successfully negotiated over $500 million in contracts and built lasting relationships, she also observed and adopted the traits of those at the top of their game. She has been featured in ESPN, Fast Company, Forbes and Sports Illustrated, and has energized organizations as diverse as AT&T, Bank of America, Michigan State, Georgia Tech, the PGA TOUR and Home Depot.

## Jason Forrest – Ch. 8

Jason Forrest is a thought leader and behavioral change expert on a mission to convince everyone he knows that they are enough! He is a sales trainer, a management coach, and the author of three books, including his latest, *Leadership Sales Coaching*. He is Chairman of the National Speakers Association's Million Dollar Speakers Group. He has been awarded Training Magazine's Top Young Trainer and a Gold Stevie Award for Sales Training Leader of the Year. He has also been awarded the top sales management program in the world. Jason is an expert at creating high-performance cultures through complete training programs. He incorporates experiential learning to increase profit, implement cultural accountability, and transform companies into high performance organizations by unleashing their human performance.

## Brad Fowler – Ch. 3, 5, 7, 8

Mr. Fowler brings extensive experience and a broad overview of the wellness industry to Nutraplex. Mr. Fowler's career has revolved around working in aggressive start-up environments, where he has established a proven track record of driving rapid growth. In 2000, he co-founded NeuroSolutions, a wholesaler of unique cognitive products in the United States and Australia and later expanded ecommerce worldwide. During this time, he became ingrained in the inner workings of the healthcare industry, and recognized some inherent flaws that he thought could be leveraged into opportunities.

In 2003, he co-founded Welnia, a wellness management software application company where he was the Director of Product Development, designing the operational platform as well as implementing various programs.

In 2008 he held a position with Salba Nutritionals as the Vice President of Operations where he designed and implemented their operational platform from the ground up. With Salba he managed all aspects of operating the company including procurement, manufacturing, quality control, R&D, product development, inventory, fulfillment, and shipping. Mr. Fowler was instrumental in integrating Salba into several national natural foods chains and mass market retailers.

Mr. Fowler currently owns and operates Benetivia® and Nutraplex®. Benetivia® is a line of nutrition supplements sold primarily through ecommerce. Nutraplex® whole body vibration machines are the ultimate health and wellness solution. Harnessing the power of Whole Body Vibration, Nutraplex® developed a quicker, safer and more effective method of putting the human body in an ideal health state where it recovers and heals much quicker than other methods used by traditional health and wellness providers.

Mr. Fowler earned a B.S. in Economics with a minor in Business and Communications from Rollins College.

## Martin Grunburg – Ch. 4, 7

Martin is the creator/inventor of The Habit Factor® as well as the author of the international bestselling book sharing the same name. He's widely recognized as the father of the modern habit tracking movement for goal achievement.

Martin presented these revolutionary insights about habit and goal achievement at TEDx in the United Arab Emirates, and his work has been featured in the world's most popular productivity blogs such as Lifehacker.com and Mashable.com as well as New York Times, C|Net and OpenForum. He's been identified by Success Magazine as one of today's most inspirational, creative and respected thought-leaders in the multibillion-dollar personal development arena.

Prior to developing and authoring The Habit Factor®, Martin has been a partner in C3 Networx, formerly Home2Office Computing Solutions, Inc. As founder/COO, he's been nominated twice for the Entrepreneur of the Year award and has twice led his team to win the Better Business Bureau Torch Award for Marketplace Ethics.

Martin served on the board of Big Brothers Big Sisters regionally in San Diego (2006 - 2016) and has been a big brother for more than 15 years. He has also served as a volunteer instructor for Junior Achievement, teaching "Success Skills" to some of the city's more economically challenged high schools.

## Rob LaBreche – Ch. 2, 7, 8

Rob LeBreche is the founder and CEO of iGrad, an award winning financial wellness company specializing in working with businesses and colleges to help foster financial literacy efforts for their employees and students. Prior to iGrad, Mr. LaBreche was the President of Consumer Marketing for College Loan Corporation, a leading lender of student loans. Mr. LaBreche was most recently recognized as a "Most

Admired CEO" by the San Diego Business Journal and is on the board of several other organizations including Holding Hands Charities, a not-for-profit he founded to assist San Diegans in need.

## Don Langmo – Ch. 1, 2, 4, 7, 8

Don Langmo is the founder and CEO of two of America's largest healthcare recruiting firms (Healthcare Support Staffing and Healthcare Scouts). Healthcare Support Staffing is an Inc. 500 award winner and the two firms have combined revenue in the $100 million range.

Don was also the founder and long-time CEO for the CSI Companies which is now part of an international recruiting organization which has sales in excess of $1 billion. The CSI Companies also was an Inc. 500 award winner under Don's leadership.

Don Langmo is a father of six and he is highly active in his local community serving on the boards of his local church, school, and little league organizations as well as actively supporting many other local not-for-profits.

## Sharon Lechter – Ch. 7

Sharon Lechter is an entrepreneur, author, philanthropist, international speaker, licensed CPA and Chartered Global Management Accountant. A life-long education advocate, she is the founder and CEO of Pay Your Family First, a financial education organization and Chief Abundance Officer for EBW2020, an organization dedicated to Empowering a Billion Women by 2020. Sharon has combined her expertise as a CPA and an international bestselling author with her unmatched passion for financial literacy and entrepreneurship to inspire change for individuals and businesses across the globe for over 30 years. Credited as the genius behind the Rich Dad brand,

Sharon is currently partnered with the Napoleon Hill Foundation. As a driving force behind these two mega brands, Sharon has demonstrated her entrepreneurial vision and business expertise while empowering audiences with messages of hope and prosperity. Sharon is also the author of the bestselling books *Think and Grow Rich for Women, Outwitting the Devil, Three Feet From Gold,* and *Rich Dad Poor Dad.* For her unparalleled commitment to community and professional excellence, Sharon was honored as the 2015 Financial Educator of the Year by the National Financial Educators Council. Her *Your Financial Mastery* college curriculum also received the Excellence in Financial Literacy Education (EIFLE) Award for 2015 "Book of the Year" from the Institute for Financial Literacy. Sharon lives each day in pursuit of and to inspire others to achieve a life of success and significance.

## Larry Linne – Forward, Ch. 3, 4

Larry G. Linne is one of the business world's most innovative thinkers. Known for making the complex simple, Larry's powerful thinking strategies combined with his broad and varied experiences has led to a significant, far-reaching career. From pro football player to CEO of multiple companies to published author, Larry speaks to thousands of business leaders each year who run world-class organizations. His ideas and training tools have been implemented in businesses of all classifications, ranging from small businesses to Fortune 100 companies. Larry is CEO of InCite Performance Group, a private client group and membership program for the top Independent Insurance Agencies and Brokerages. He also is a Partner in Bushido Captive Innovations LLC, a captive insurance consulting firm, and is founder and Chairman of Intellectual Innovations, an executive development company. When Larry is not advising and delivering keynote presentations, you can find him in his backyard, the Rocky Mountains, competing in mountain bike and Cyclocross races, along with spending time on his ranch with his family. He is married to Deborah and has five daughters.

## Travis Medley – Ch. 6

Travis Medley is a staffing industry expert and lover of theme parks turned entrepreneur. Travis founded TalentZök, a specialized recruitment firm based in San Diego consistently on the list of fastest growing businesses and best places to work. In addition to being a father of triplets, he wrote the definitive English-language guide to Tokyo Disneyland entitled *Travelers Series Guide to Tokyo Disneyland* and *Tokyo Disney Sea.*

## Steve Mehr – Ch. 2, 3, 6

Steve Mehr is an entrepreneur, start-up expert, lawyer, media company CEO, speaker, author and motivator, specializing in teaching people how to build and scale their business. He has founded, built, and sold over a dozen businesses across a variety of fields.

After achieving success at an early age he now acts as a mentor, coach, and advisor helping other entrepreneurs learn from his legal and business experience.

## Anthony Mongeluzo – Ch. 3

Anthony Mongeluzo is a serial entrepreneur, a top gun computer expert and CEO/President of PCS www.helpmepcs.com. In 2002, at the age of 22 and with no outside capital, he founded Pro Computer Service (PCS) in his parents' home. He was literally "home alone" as he started to position PCS in the burgeoning IT market.

Today, his IT firm operates in five states (New Jersey, Pennsylvania, Delaware, Maryland) and recently opened a

Washington, D.C. office. Local and national media have consistently rated PCS as one of the fastest-growing firms in the country. He owns four other companies and cruises to meetings daily in the #TechTank, a one-of-a-kind mobile office.

Anthony is FOX-TV's IT expert in Philadelphia. National, regional and local media frequently call upon him for his expertise and opinion on IT and small-business issues. A small sampling of these media outlets includes: The Wall Street Journal, The Associated Press, On the Record with Greta Van Susteren, FOX News, ABC, NBC, MSN, MSNBC, CNBC, the Philadelphia Business Journal and Courier-Post (New Jersey).

Despite his status as a personality within the IT and business community, he started as a computer technician, earning more than 10 industry certifications from both Microsoft and CompTIA.

### Cameron Morrissey – Ch. 1, 5

One of the most popular thought leaders in management and leadership, Cameron Morrissey is a real world manager offering advice from his 20+ years of management experience daily to over 1,000,000 subscribers to his blog and social media channels. An author, speaker and coach, his books on leadership include *The Manager's Diary*, *The Manager's Diary* II, and *The 7 Deadly Sins of Leadership*.

### Austin Netzley – Ch. 3, 6, 7

Austin Netzley helps business owners use their book to establish expert positioning and scale their business. He is the Founder and CEO of "Epic Launch", a leading book marketing company working with many of today's top thought leaders which has helped authors move over 1,000,000 books globally. Austin is a former collegiate athlete and the #1 international bestselling author of *Make Money, Live Wealthy*, which has been downloaded and sold over 60,000 times. He is also the co-creator of 6 Months to 6 Figures, helping starting entrepreneurs get to their first $100k as quickly as possible. Austin has been featured on many of the world's largest business websites and is a regular contributor to Business Insider.

## Rob Neville – Ch. 6

Mr. Rob Neville is one of the founders of Savara and has served as CEO and President since 2008. Savara is developing treatments for rare respiratory diseases such as cystic fibrosis and pulmonary alveolar proteinases. Prior to Savara, Mr. Neville was founder and CEO of Evity, Inc., which was acquired by BMC Software. Based on his work at Evity and Savara, Mr. Neville was honored as a two-time finalist for the Ernst & Young Entrepreneur of the Year award. Mr. Neville holds a post-graduate Engineering degree from the University of Natal South Africa.

## Sujan Patel – Ch. 6

Sujan Patel is the co-founder of Web Profits, a growth marketing agency helping companies leverage the latest and greatest marketing strategy to fuel their businesses. He has over 13 years of internet marketing experience and has led the digital marketing strategy for companies like Sales Force, Mint, Intuit and many other Fortune 500 caliber companies. Sujan took everything he learned in his career and wrote a book to help marketers with growth with his book *100 Days of Growth* which has sold over 37,000 copies last year alone.

## Andre Phillipe van den Broeck – Ch. 1, 4

André Phillipe van den Broeck created Andre' Phillipe, Inc. which is a luxury, lifestyle brand that is centered around men's fashion and provides the unique opportunity to build a true community around its companies unlike any other fashion brand in existence. With a keen sense of classic fashion, a network of committed service providers, and world class branding, marketing and advertising acumen, Andre' Phillipe, Inc. and its subsidiaries are positioned to expand its business and broaden its organizational reach in a superbly powerful, effective, and profitable way.

Along with being the Founder and Chief Executive Officer of André Phillipe Inc., André also serves as a Marketing and Branding consultant for companies both regional and global in size. He serves on various advisory boards and board of directors and is the Marketing Chair of the Music and Memories Gala that takes place in Austin, TX. He's married with two wonderful children and lives in the Dallas suburb of Prosper, TX.

## Marc Randolph – Ch. 6

Marc Randolph is a veteran Silicon Valley entrepreneur, advisor and investor. Marc was co-founder of the online movie and television streaming service Netflix, serving as their founding CEO, as the executive producer of their web site, and as a member of their board of directors until his retirement from Netflix in 2004.

Although best known for starting Netflix, Marc's career as an entrepreneur spans more than four decades. He's been a founder of more than half a dozen other successful start-ups, a mentor to scores of early stage entrepreneurs, and an investor in numerous successful tech ventures (and an even larger number of unsuccessful ones).

Most recently, Marc co-founded analytics software company Looker Data Sciences, and currently serves as an advisor to five other startups, serving variously as a mentor, CEO coach, and/or board member.

He is a frequent speaker at industry events, works extensively with young entrepreneur programs, and is a trustee of the non-profit National Outdoor Leadership School and the environmental advocacy group One Percent For The Planet.

Marc is charming, handsome and modest; and whenever possible avoids referring to himself in the third person. He lives in Santa Cruz, California.


**Nick Ruiz – Ch. 6, 7, 8**

Nick Ruiz is a TWICE self-made entrepreneur who quickly bounced back into financial independence from bankruptcy. He teaches people how to create success from scratch and you can visit him at NickRuiz.tv or AlphaHomeFlipping.com


**Emily Schaller – Ch. 6, 7**

Equal parts spark, wit and humor, Emily is claiming her victories against cystic fibrosis having launched the Rock CF Foundation to heighten public awareness and raise funds to increase the quality of life for everyone with CF. Emily created and manages an internationally acclaimed line of merchandise to help fulfill the mission of Rock CF. Today, Emily's battle against this deadly genetic disease is printed in Runner's World, FORBES, The Atlantic and SPIN magazines, the New York Times, The Washington Post, USA Today, NPR and posted on Competitor.com, Shape.com, the Associated Press, and various cystic fibrosis focused educational websites. She is a super teacher and a speaker, addressing parents, patients and audiences about the effects of cystic fibrosis and the ever changing and improving treatments being made. Through

Emily's humor and personal experience, she inspires the masses to transform their lives with exercise, diet and goal setting.

## Jeff Shelton – Ch. 2, 3, 7, 8, 9

Jeff Shelton is an award winning CEO, venture capitalist, business advisor, and entrepreneur. He is the founder and owner of Wholesale Warranties, a leading provider of direct to consumer of auto, RV, and powersport extended warranty protection services. Jeff discovered entrepreneurship during his 20's while living in his hometown in Minnesota before relocating to San Diego to pursue his career. Currently, he co-owns and advises several enterprises including: Eagle Creative Media, a digital marketing and videography company; RiverMarinas.com, a marine dealership conglomerate; and Landmark Makers, a recruiting firm dedicated to talent acquisition strategies and implementation for high-growth companies.

In 2016 Jeff was named a finalist for the San Diego Business Journal's Most Admired CEO award. In his spare time, he works with various charities to advance CF research and improve the lives of orphans in Mexico. He also participates in mentoring programs to help develop the next generator of innovators and entrepreneurs. Currently, he lives in San Diego with the love of his life, Klyn Elsbury.

## Louis Spagnuolo – Ch. 4, 6, 7

Louis Spagnuolo is a serial entrepreneur and serves as the Chief Executive Officer for Don't Look Media LLC, a highly recognized privately held Internet Monetization Company.

During his career Louis Spagnuolo has worked with Professional Athletes, Entertainers, National Business Leaders, Heads of State and countless genuinely fantastic people, while sharing in the financial dreams of all his clients to the tune of over $884 Million in deal participations.

Louis Spagnuolo has been recognized in over 278 major media publications such as Forbes Magazine, The South Florida Business Journal, The Palm Beach Post, The Sun-Sentinel, South Florida Business Leader Magazine, Fox Business News, BankRate.com, South Florida Opulence and The Associated Press. Louis Spagnuolo is a nationally sought after expert in Internet Monetization, with an emphasis on asset acquisitions that can be leveraged to generate liquidity events.

In 2015, Don't Look Media was proud to announce its 14th liquidity event, through the sale of its online insurance subsidiary www.CancerInsurance.com.

### Beth Sufian – Ch. 2, 7

Beth Sufian is a partner in the law firm of Sufian & Passamano, LLP in Houston, Texas. Over the past 26 years, Beth has focused her practice on advocating for the rights of people with chronic illness around the country.

Beth is the Director of the Cystic Fibrosis Legal Information Hotline which has provided legal information to over 45,000 people in the Cystic Fibrosis community since 1998. Beth is also the Director of the Cystic Fibrosis Social Security Project which has successfully represented close to 2,000 people in obtaining Social Security benefits.

Sufian has spoken at 120 hospitals around the country and published over 20 articles in national medical journals.

Beth is also a member of the Board of Directors for the United States Adult CF Association. She has received numerous awards recognizing her work including an award from Time Magazine, the Cystic Fibrosis Foundation, Baylor College of Medicine and Cystic Fibrosis Research Inc.

## Nick Talbot – Ch. 7

Nick Talbot is CEO of the IVSC. In his spare time he raises profile and money for Cystic Fibrosis charities in the hope of making a small contribution to helping move towards more medical breakthroughs. As part of this, Nick was lucky to survive the two worst natural disasters to hit Everest in 2014 and 2015 before becoming the first person with CF to summit Everest.

## Christina Waters - Ch. 7

Dr. Christina Waters' passion lies in implementing innovative approaches to improve global healthcare of patients that are in the most need. She is CEO and Founder of RARE Science, a non-profit research organization, that accelerates finding therapies for kids with rare and undiagnosed diseases by empowering patient families/foundations with tools to identify more immediate therapeutic solutions. From international experience at Genomics Institute of the Novartis Research Institute, aTyr, Cell Therapeutics sede secondaria, and a Senior Advisor for Personalized Medicine and Health Informatics for Pricewaterhouse Coopers' Personalized Medicine and Health Sciences Practices she also serves as a strategic consultant for academic and research organizations across the healthcare continuum.

As a supporter of women in life science, she also is a mentor at the Zahn Innovation Platform Launchpad at San Diego State University for women student entrepreneurs and also serves as a Scientific Advisory board member, for Global Genes|Rare Project, which focuses on advocacy and education for the rare disease community.

## Ric Groeber – Co-Producer and Editor

Ric Groeber is a master at innovation, hard worker, and living life to its fullest. He is an accomplished engineer, business strategist, editor, and entrepreneur. Ric grew up in Cinnaminson, NJ and studied Mechanical, Aerospace and Biomechanical Engineering at Rutgers University. Later, he obtained his MBA from the University of Florida.

Professionally, Ric Groeber started out his career as a dishwasher at a restaurant two blocks from his house, and has worked his way into many different fields including, Mergers and Acquisitions Project Management, Nuclear Generator Engineering, and of course, Entrepreneurship. He is currently the CEO and founder of Groeber Enterprises, specializing in real-estate management and entrepreneurial consulting. Additionally, Ric has appeared on MTV and BuzzFeed, and once ran a half-marathon dressed as a princess in support of curing childhood cancer. He currently resides in Orlando, FL.

# Acknowledgements

127 hours. Danny Boyle. Fox Searchlight Pictures. 2010.

Akalp, Nellie. "Entrepreneurs Beware: Persistence (not patience) is a Virtue". Mashable.com. June 23, 2015.

Colvin, Geoff. Talent is Overrated: What Really Separates World-Class Performers from Everybody Else. Portfolio. 2010.

Corley, Thomas C. Rich Habits – The Daily Success Habits of Wealthy Individuals. Langdon Street Press. 2010.

Eat Pray Love. Ryan Murphy. Columbia Pictures. 2010

Freeman, Mike. "How Gary Vaynerchuk Built His Empire". Shopify.com. September 15, 2011.
Gates, Bill. The Road Ahead. Viking. 1995

Gilbert, Elizabeth. Eat, Pray, Love: One Woman's Search for Everything Across Italy, India and Indonesia. Riverhead Books. 2007.

Gladwell, Malcolm. Outliers: The Story of Success. Back Bay Books. 2011.

Grant, Adam. Give and Take: Why Helping Others Drives Our Success. Penguin Books. 2014.

Hardy, Darren. The Compound Effect. Vanguard Press. 2010.

Hudson, Paul. "100 Top Entrepreneurs Who Succeeded Without a College Degree". EliteDaily.com. March 13, 2013.

Merriam-Webster. The Merriam-Webster Dictionary. Merriam-Webster, Inc. 2007.

Rackham, Neil. SPIN Selling. McGraw-Hill. 1988.

Ralston, Aron. Between a Rock and a Hard Place. Atria Books. 2004.

Tracy, Brian. Focal Point: A Proven System to Simplify Your Life, Double Your Productivity, and Achieve All Your Goals. AMACOM. 2004.

United States. Senate. U.S. Senate Special Committee on Aging & the Senate Committee on Small Business and Entrepreneurship. Stangler, Diane. In Search of a Second Act: The Challenges and Advantages of Senior Entrepreneurship. February 12, 2014.

U.S. Census Bureau, 2010 Census Brief, Age and Sex Composition: 2010. May 2011.

Wood, Glenice. Davidson, Marilyn. Fielden, Sandra. Minorities in Entrepreneurship: An International Review. Edward Elgar Pub. 2012.

# About The Author

**Klyn Elsbury** is an inspirational speaker, CEO, and Entrepreneur. At a young age, she was diagnosed with the genetic killer, Cystic Fibrosis. Even from the beginning of her life, she never let it define her. Growing up in a small town in Iowa, she was constantly surprising both her doctors and her parents with her energy, optimism, intelligence, and lust for life.

Despite her hospitalizations, medications, nebulizers, and a severely plummeting lung function that required spending up to six months a year on IV treatments (usually in the hospital) she graduated from Iowa Western Community College with a 4.0 GPA and on scholarship, she enrolled in Iowa State University.

However, she soon realized that due to her life-limiting situation, her future could be better spent pursuing more efficient accomplishments. She dropped out and moved to Orlando to pursue a career in recruiting and to focus on her health. During this period, Klyn turned to some of the most influential authors of the time including Darren Hardy, Napoleon Hill, Rick Pitino, Larry Winget, Malcolm Gladwell, Robert Kiyosaki and Sharon Lechter. These books changed her life, and convinced her that she had more to live for than simply living as long as possible.

She eventually moved to San Diego in order to be closer to the industry that was developing the very drugs that she would need to survive. Living in San Diego, she met tons of entrepreneurs, athletes, and overall influential people. She quickly immersed herself in their world, eager to learn as much about their mindset as possible. Despite her illness, she became a motivational speaker, and helped to found Landmark Makers, a full-services recruiting firm dedicated to helping high-growth companies with talent acquisition strategies and implementation.

Klyn Elsbury shares the knowledge she gained from these entrepreneurs, athletes, and influencers of the world in "*I AM ___: The Untold Story of Success*". Through this book she explores the true habits, stories, and mindsets of ordinary people that have achieved extraordinary things. She shows that all of us possess the very qualities needed to become successful as long as we are willing to learn, confront failure, and put the effort into self-improvement (which you have already done by buying this book!)

Made in the USA
Middletown, DE
20 December 2016